HISTORY OF NORTH AFRICA

THE DIAGRAM GROUP

Facts On File, Inc.

History of Africa: History of North Africa
Copyright © 2003 by The Diagram Group

Diagram Visual Information Ltd

Editorial director:	Denis Kennedy
Editor:	Peter Harrison
Contributor:	Simon Adams
Consultant:	Keith Lye
Indexer:	Martin Hargreaves
Senior designer:	Lee Lawrence
Designers:	Claire Bojczuk, Gill Shaw
Illustrators:	Kathy McDougall, Graham Rosewarne
Research:	Neil McKenna, Patricia Robertson

Facts On File, Inc.
132 West 31st Street
New York NY 10001

Library of Congress Cataloging-in-Publication Data
History of North Africa / the Diagram Group.
     p. cm. – (History of Africa)
   Includes bibliographical references and index.
   ISBN 0-8160-5060-0 (set) – ISBN 0-8160-5061-9
   1. Africa, North–History. I. Diagram Group. II. Series.

DT167 .H57 2003
961–dc21
                                    2002035207

Facts On File books are available at special discounts when purchased in bulk quantities for businesses, associations, institutions, or sales promotions. Please call our Special Sales Department in New York at 212/967-8800 or 800/322-8755.

You can find Facts On File on the World Wide Web at: http://www.factsonfile.com

Printed in the United States of America

EB DIAG 10 9 8 7 6 5 4 3 2 1

Contents

FOREWORD

The six-volume History of Africa series has been designed as a companion set to the Peoples of Africa series. Although, of necessity, there is some overlap between the two series, there is also a significant shift in focus. Whereas Peoples of Africa focuses on ethnographic issues, that is the the individual human societies which make up the continent, History of Africa graphically presents a historical overview of the political forces that shaped the vast continent today.

History of North Africa starts off with a description of the region in depth, including its religions, land, climate, and the languages spoken there today, with particular relevance to the colonial legacy as it affected the spoken word region-by-region. There then follows an overview of events from prehistory to the present day, and a brief discussion of the various historical sources that help us to learn about the past.

The major part of the book comprises an in-depth examination of the history of the region from the first humans through the early civilizations or chiefdoms; the development of trade with other countries; the arrival of European colonists, and the effect this had on the indigenous peoples; the struggles for independence in the last century; and the current political situation in the nation, or island, states in the 21st century.

Interspersed throughout the book are special features on a variety of political topics or historical themes which bring the region to life, such as Carthaginian gods and the afterlife, the Barbary pirates, the Ottoman Empire, the Mahdist rebellion in Sudan, and the Algerian Civil War.

Throughout the book the reader will also find timelines which list major events combined with maps, diagrams and illustrations, presented in two color throughout, which help to explain these events in more detail, and place them within the context of world events. Finally, there is a glossary which defines unfamiliar words used in the book, and a comprehensive index. Taken together with the other five volumes in this series, *History of North Africa* will provide the reader with a memorable snapshot of Africa as a continent with an enormously rich history.

Dates

In this book, we use the dating system BCE – Before Common Era – and CE – Common Era. 1 CE is the same year as 1 AD. We have used this system because the majority of people in North Africa are Muslim and do not recognize the system BC – Before Christ – and AD – Anno Domini – which is a Christian dating system.

The religions of North Africa

The vast majority of people in North Africa are Muslim. Islam, the religion of Muslims, was founded by the prophet Muhammad in Arabia in the early seventh century CE. After Muhammad's death in 632, Arab armies swept out across the Middle East into North Africa, invading Egypt in 640 and the rest of the region by 711. Under Arab rule, most people converted to Islam. Christianity survives today in small communities in Egypt and Sudan. Tiny Jewish communities also exist in Algeria, Morocco, and Tunisia.

Tulum mosque
Built during the period 876–879, this is the oldest mosque surviving in Egypt.

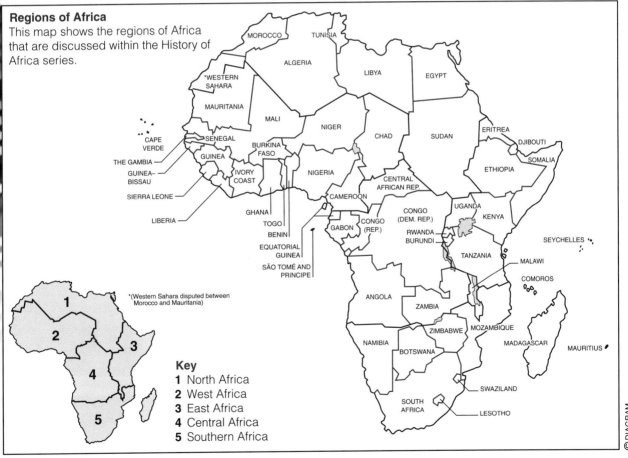

Regions of Africa
This map shows the regions of Africa that are discussed within the History of Africa series.

MOROCCO
TUNISIA
ALGERIA
LIBYA
EGYPT
*WESTERN SAHARA
MAURITANIA
MALI
NIGER
CHAD
SUDAN
ERITREA
DJIBOUTI
CAPE VERDE
SENEGAL
BURKINA FASO
THE GAMBIA
GUINEA
GUINEA-BISSAU
IVORY COAST
NIGERIA
CENTRAL AFRICAN REP.
ETHIOPIA
SOMALIA
SIERRA LEONE
CAMEROON
LIBERIA
GHANA
TOGO
BENIN
EQUATORIAL GUINEA
SÃO TOMÉ AND PRINCIPE
GABON
CONGO (REP.)
CONGO (DEM. REP.)
UGANDA
RWANDA
BURUNDI
KENYA
SEYCHELLES
TANZANIA
MALAWI
COMOROS
ANGOLA
ZAMBIA
MOZAMBIQUE
MADAGASCAR
MAURITIUS
ZIMBABWE
NAMIBIA
BOTSWANA
SWAZILAND
SOUTH AFRICA
LESOTHO

*(Western Sahara disputed between Morocco and Mauritania)

Key
1 North Africa
2 West Africa
3 East Africa
4 Central Africa
5 Southern Africa

© DIAGRAM

THE REGION

Land

North Africa consists of six countries, Algeria, Egypt, Libya, Morocco, Sudan, and Tunisia, and the disputed territory of Western Sahara. It is largely a desert region, stretching from the Atlantic Ocean in the west to the Red Sea in the east. To the north it is bordered by the Mediterranean Sea and to the south by the Sahel, a semi-desert region that fringes the Sahara and straddles the border between North and West Africa.

North Africa is divided into four main regions (below): a narrow strip of coastal lowland bordering the Atlantic Ocean and the Mediterranean Sea; the vast Saharan Plateau, which ranges from 500 to 2,000 ft (150–600 m) high and occupies much of the region; the Nile Basin, the land drained by the Nile River which flows north through Sudan and Egypt; and three mountainous areas in western Sudan, southern Algeria, and in northern Morocco and Algeria. "Sahara" is the Arabic word for desert,

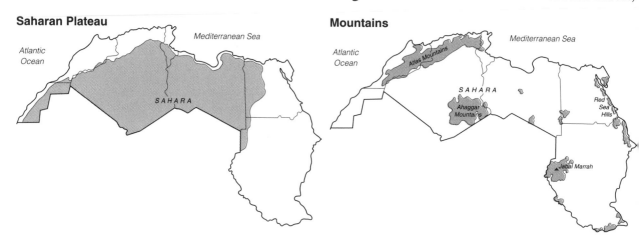

Saharan Plateau

Mountains

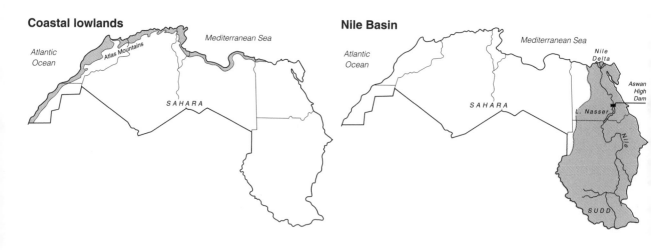

Coastal lowlands

Nile Basin

and the Saharan Plateau contains most of the world's largest desert, which stretches across almost the entire width of North Africa. Because the Sahara is very hot and dry, most people live in the Nile Basin and coastal lowlands.

Climate

The coastal regions of North Africa have a subtropical climate with mainly hot, dry summers and mild winters with moderate rainfall. South of the coastal region is a semiarid strip of land with large daily swings in temperature and light rainfall.

The Sahara has an arid climate, with extremely hot summers – often above 35 °C (95 °F) – and mild winters. Throughout the year, the temperature varies widely between day and night. Rainfall is very rare in the Sahara.

Temperature

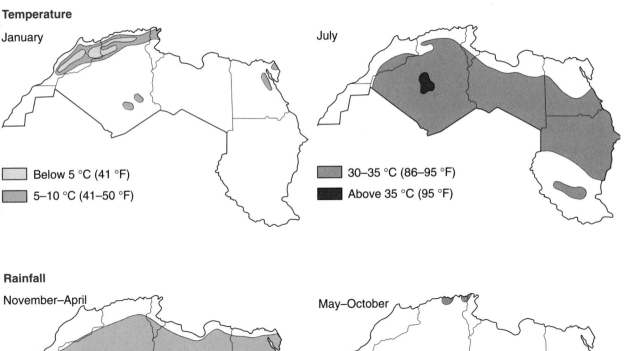

January

Below 5 °C (41 °F)
5–10 °C (41–50 °F)

July

30–35 °C (86–95 °F)
Above 35 °C (95 °F)

Rainfall

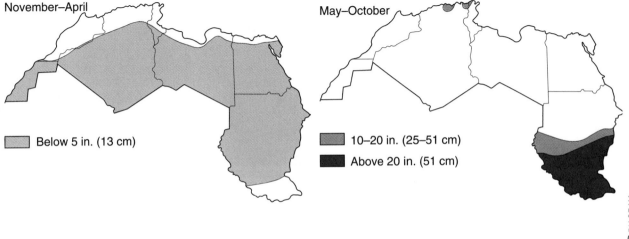

November–April

Below 5 in. (13 cm)

May–October

10–20 in. (25–51 cm)
Above 20 in. (51 cm)

© DIAGRAM

North Africa today

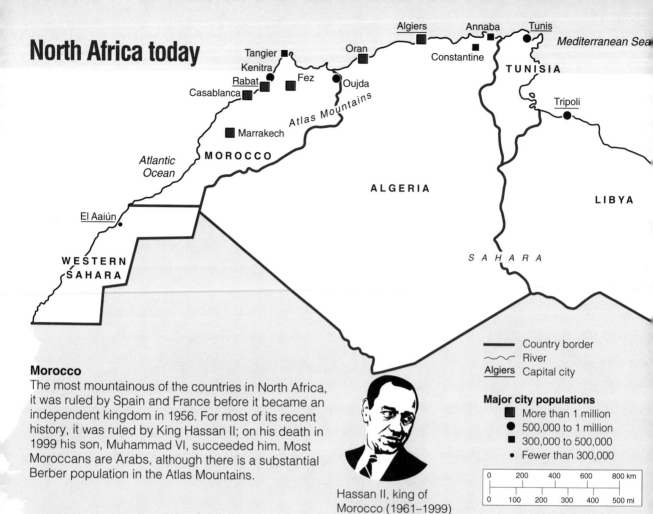

Mediterranean Sea

TUNISIA

Tripoli

MOROCCO

Atlas Mountains

Atlantic Ocean

ALGERIA

LIBYA

WESTERN SAHARA

El Aaiún

SAHARA

Algiers · Annaba · Tunis

Oran · Constantine

Tangier · Kenitra · Rabat · Fez · Oujda

Casablanca

Marrakech

——	Country border
~~	River
Algiers	Capital city

Major city populations
- ■ More than 1 million
- ● 500,000 to 1 million
- ▪ 300,000 to 500,000
- · Fewer than 300,000

0	200	400	600	800 km
0	100 200	300	400	500 mi

Morocco
The most mountainous of the countries in North Africa, it was ruled by Spain and France before it became an independent kingdom in 1956. For most of its recent history, it was ruled by King Hassan II; on his death in 1999 his son, Muhammad VI, succeeded him. Most Moroccans are Arabs, although there is a substantial Berber population in the Atlas Mountains.

Hassan II, king of Morocco (1961–1999)

Algeria
Africa's second largest country, it became independent in 1962 after a struggle against French rule, which began in 1830. The country is a republic, dominated by the army, which took power in 1992. Since then, the government has fought Islamic militants who have waged a terrorist campaign that has led to the loss of many lives. The majority of Algerians are Arabs, with small communities of Berbers and Tuaregs living in the desert and mountain regions of the south.

Ahmad Ben Bella, first president of Algeria (1963–1965)

Tunisia
The smallest state in North Africa, it gained independence from France in 1956. It then became a republic led by Habib Bourguiba until he was replaced in 1987 by Ben Ali. The government is challenged by Islamic fundamentalists who wish to establish an Islamic state. Tunisia's close proximity to Europe means that it has close links with the European Union and is a popular destination for European tourists.

Habib Bourguiba, first prime minister of Tunisia (1957–1987)

Western Sahara
In 1975 the Spanish agreed to divide their colony of Spanish Sahara between Morocco and Mauritania and withdrew in December. However, in early 1976 the Polisario Front declared Western Sahara, as it then became, to be independent. Polisario remains in exile today. Mauritania withdrew its claim to the south of the country in 1979, leaving Morocco in full control. It then built a huge defensive wall around the east and south of the country. In 1988 the

Benghazi

Alexandria Port Said

Suez Canal

Giza ■ Suez

Cairo

EGYPT

S A H A R A

Nile

Red Sea

Aswan High Dam

Lake Nasser

Port Sudan •

Nile

Omdurman ●

● Khartoum

SUDAN

White Nile

Blue Nile

Bahr al Jabal (Nile)

Population density:
people per sq. mile (sq. km)
- Fewer than 5 (2)
- 5–25 (2–10)
- 25–100 (10–40)
- 100–500 (40–200)
- More than 500 (200)

Egypt
In this, the most populous country in North Africa, the vast majority of people are Arabs, with a sizeable minority of Coptic Christians. The country gained its independence from Britain in 1922 and at first was a monarchy. In 1952 the monarchy was overthrown and Egypt became a republic. The country is politically stable, although militant Islamic groups are seeking to turn the country into a Muslim state.

Hosni Mubarak, president of Egypt, 1981

Sudan
Africa's largest country, it is divided between an Arab north and a black African south. An independent republic since 1956, it has often been ruled by the army. Attempts to impose Islamic law have caused civil war since independence, despite attempts to reach a peaceful settlement.

Omar al-Bashir, president of Sudan since 1993

Libya
Although mostly inhospitable desert, it is the wealthiest country in the region because of its vast resources of oil and natural gas. It became an independent kingdom in 1951 after 30 years of Italian rule and then, after World War II, British and French occupation. In 1969 the monarchy was overthrown by Colonel Muammar al-Quaddafi who still runs the country today.

Muammar al-Quaddafi, leader of Libya since 1969

United Nations arranged a ceasefire between Morocco and the Polisario Front, which came into force in 1991. However, a referendum on the future of the country was promised in 1992 but has still not taken place.

© DIAGRAM

The languages of North Africa

The six countries of North Africa are all populated by Arabs, and Arabic is therefore the official language in each country. Arabic is a Semitic language, a group that also includes Hebrew and the Ethiopian languages of Amharic and Tigrinya. There are many different forms of Arabic.

Colloquial, or spoken, Arabic varies from country to country, and region to region. The Arabic spoken in Morocco is different from that spoken in Sudan. Written Arabic, however, descends directly from the classical Arabic language of the Qur'an, the Islamic holy book, and is the standard written language of all Arabs. Classical Arabic is now only used in the Qur'an, but its spoken form, modern standard Arabic, is used on radio, television, movies and in communications between Arabs who speak different forms of colloquial Arabic.

Arabic script
Arabic must be read from left to right: most of the symbols are consonants, and vowels are indicated by marks which are called diacritics, above or below the letters.

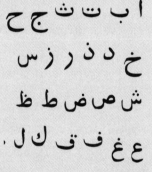

Kufic style
Of the two main styles of Arabic script, Nashki and Kufic, the latter shown on this Persian tankard was most popular in the early years of Islam. From the 11th century onwards, Nashki became more popular.

Local languages
Across North Africa, local people all speak their own languages. The Berbers of Algeria and Morocco speak Berber, an ancient language related to Ancient Egyptian but written in Arabic script. Berber has more than 20 different dialects, of which three are commonly used in each country. Most Berbers also speak Arabic, French, or Spanish. In both Algeria and Morocco, Berber is the officially recognized second language.

The Tuaregs of Algeria and Libya also speak a Berber language called Tamacheq; it has four main dialects, which are mutually intelligible. Tuaregs often call themselves Kel Tamacheq, "people of the Tamacheq language."

In Egypt, the Copts speak a version of Ancient Egyptian enriched with Greek words. It is written in a script derived from the Greek alphabet. The Coptic language was the last form of Ancient Egyptian to be used. After the Arab conquest of Egypt in 640 CE, it was replaced by Arabic and, by the 14th century, survived only in the services of the Coptic Christian church. Today, Arabic is used for parts of these services, and Copts now use Arabic as their first language.

The colonial legacy
Because the countries of North Africa were all once colonized by Europeans, European languages are common throughout the region.

French is widely spoken in Morocco, Algeria, and Tunisia, while Spanish is still spoken in the main towns of Morocco and Western Sahara. Both French and English are spoken in Egypt; because of its international dominance, English is rapidly becoming the second language throughout the region.

African languages

The people of Africa speak more than 1,000 different languages, most of them "home" languages native to the continent. The remaining languages, such as Arabic, English, or French, have all been introduced by settlers or invaders from Asia or Europe. The home languages are divided into four main families, within which are several subfamilies. These are then divided into groups and again into subgroups. Those languages spoken in North Africa are printed in *italic* type below.

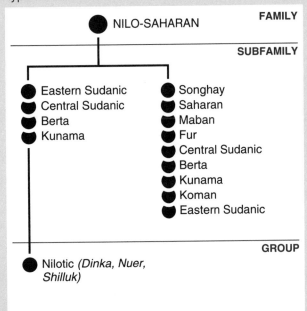

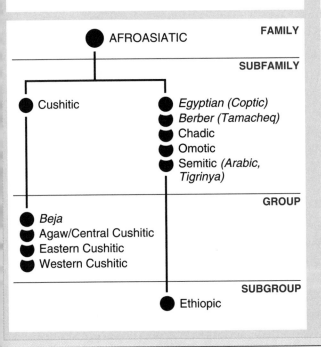

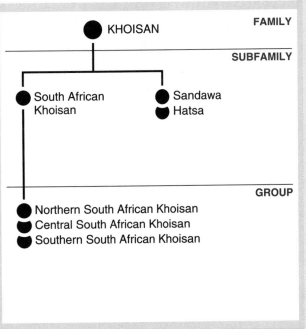

THE HISTORY

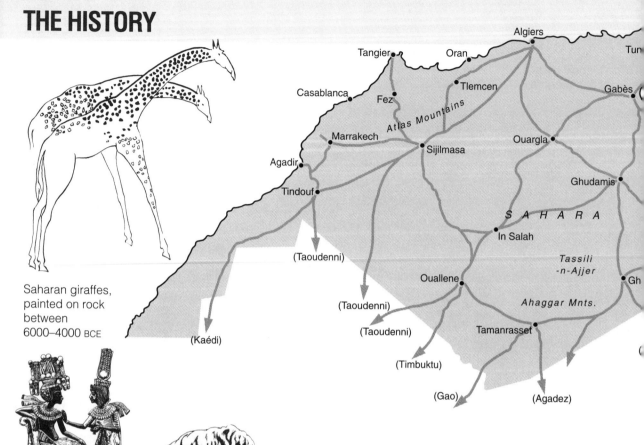

Saharan giraffes, painted on rock between 6000–4000 BCE

Tutankhamun, the Egyptian pharaoh, and his wife

Alexander the Great, liberator of Egypt from Persian rule

Septimus Severus, emperor of Rome, and Caracalla

A naval invasion of Spain by Muslims between 700–1200 CE

We know about the history of North Africa from a large number of different sources. Ancient buildings, such as tombs, temples, and pyramids, and vast numbers of artifacts tell us about the early civilizations of the Nile Valley, while paintings on the rocks of Tassili-n-Ajjer, Algeria, depict life in the Sahara thousands of years ago, when the area was fertile and well-watered.

The many invaders and settlers in North Africa, from the Berbers and Phoenicians through the Greeks and Romans to the Arabs, Ottomans, and European colonialists have all left a record of buildings and artifacts, as have the various civilizations and dynasties that have ruled the region over the past 3,000 years.

Explorers such as the 14th-century Arab traveller Ibn Battuta, and many more recent adventurers, left written records of their journeys around and across the Sahara Desert, while many documents and scholarly works of history and record have been preserved in libraries, mosques, churches, and monasteries.

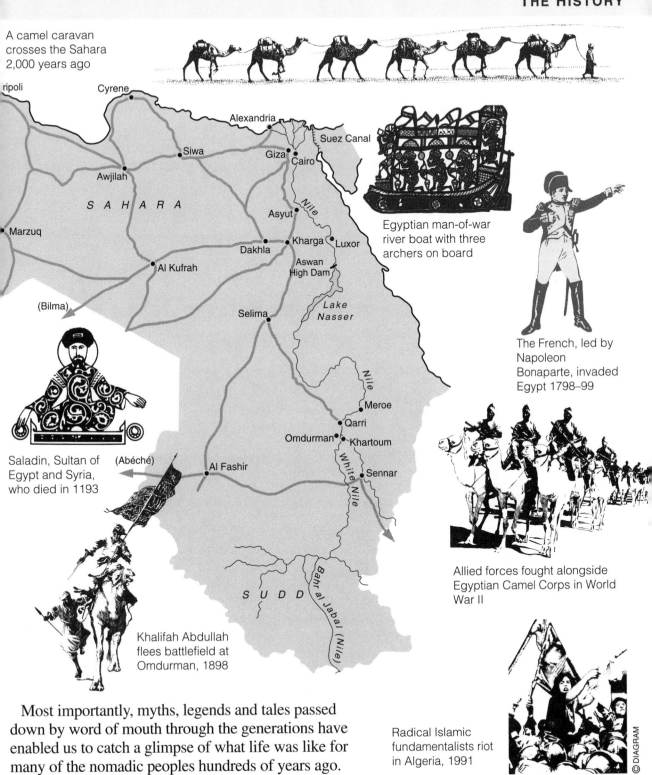

A camel caravan crosses the Sahara 2,000 years ago

Egyptian man-of-war river boat with three archers on board

The French, led by Napoleon Bonaparte, invaded Egypt 1798–99

Saladin, Sultan of Egypt and Syria, who died in 1193

Khalifah Abdullah flees battlefield at Omdurman, 1898

Allied forces fought alongside Egyptian Camel Corps in World War II

Radical Islamic fundamentalists riot in Algeria, 1991

Map labels:
ripoli · Cyrene · Alexandria · Suez Canal · Siwa · Giza · Cairo · Awjilah · SAHARA · Nile · Asyut · Marzuq · Kharga · Luxor · Dakhla · Aswan High Dam · Al Kufrah · (Bilma) · Lake Nasser · Selima · Nile · Meroe · Qarri · Omdurman · Khartoum · (Abéché) · Al Fashir · Sennar · White Nile · SUDD · Bahr al Jabal (Nile)

Most importantly, myths, legends and tales passed down by word of mouth through the generations have enabled us to catch a glimpse of what life was like for many of the nomadic peoples hundreds of years ago.

© DIAGRAM

Events

NORTH AFRICAN EVENTS	WORLD EVENTS

To 3200 BCE

c.4.4 mya *Australopithecus ramidus* evolves in East Africa

c.2 mya *Homo habilis* evolves in East Africa

c.1.6 mya *Homo erectus* replaces *Homo habilis*

c.400,000 BCE *Homo sapiens sapiens* emerges in southern Africa

c.35,000 *Homo sapiens sapiens* settles in whole of Africa

c.20,000–10,000 Ice Age turns North Africa dry and hot

c.8500 First people resettle the Sahara

c.7000 First pottery made in the Sahara

c.6000 Rock art created in the Sahara

c.4500 Cattle domesticated in the Sahara

c.4500 Settled villages emerge in Nile Valley

c.4000 Sahara begins to dry out

c.3500 Ancient Egyptians develop copper and later bronze-making skills

c.3300 First walled towns built in Egypt

c.3200 Nubian kingdom of Kush emerges (Egypt/Sudan)

World events:

c.850,000 First hominids reach Europe from Africa

c.120,000 Neanderthals in Europe

c.30,000 Earliest cave art in France and Spain

c.3500 Wheel and plow invented

c.3500–2300 Sumerian civilization (Iraq)

3201–1070 BCE

c.3050 Egyptian kingdom established

c.3000 Berbers settle on coast from Morocco to Egypt

c.2630 First step pyramid built in Egypt

c.2528 Great Pyramid of Khufu and the Sphinx built in Egypt

1750–1500 Kush at its greatest extent

c.1500 Egypt conquers Kush

c.1300 Temples of Ramesses II and Nefertiti built in Egypt

1070 Egypt enters period of decline

World events:

c.3000–1500 Indus Valley civilization (India/Pakistan)

c.1600–1200 Greek Mycenaean civilization

c.1200 Beginnings of Judaism

1069–30 CE

c.920 Kingdom of Nubia established at Napata (Egypt/Sudan)

814 City-state of Carthage founded (Tunisia)

750 Greek Empire extends along North African coast

671–653 Assyrians rule Egypt

525–404 Persians conquer and rule Egypt

332–304 Macedonians (Greeks) rule Egypt

304 Ptolemaic dynasty founded in Egypt

c.300 Nubia transfers capital from Napata to Meroe (Sudan)

264–146 Three Punic Wars between Carthage and Rome

c.250 Three Berber kingdoms established in northwest

205 Ptolemaic Egypt reaches greatest extent

146 Romans destroy Carthage

30 CE Romans assume control of Egypt

World events:

c.1000 Hindu Rig-Veda sacred text completed

c.1000 Agriculture established in North American Great Basin

776 First Olympic Games in Greece

c563 Birth of Buddha

509 Republic of Rome established

334–323 Alexander the Great creates Macedonian empire

c.320 Indian Gupta dynasty begun

300 Great Wall of China begun

c30 CE Jesus crucified; start of Christianity

29 CE–632

27 Roman Republic becomes an Empire under Augustus

285 Romans abandon much of northwest Africa

324 Meroitic kingdom conquered by Axumite kingdom

429 Vandals from Europe invade North Africa

World events:

c.300 Rise of Mayan civilization in what is now Mexico

395 Roman Empire split into two parts

455 Vandals sack Rome

NORTH AFRICAN EVENTS	**WORLD EVENTS**
533 Vandals conquered by Byzantine (Eastern Roman) empire	**622** Muhammad's flight from Mecca to Medina **624** T'ang dynasty unites China **632** Death of Muhammad

633–1000

640 Arabs invade Egypt **711** Ommayad Arabs control whole of North Africa **711** Ommayad army invades Spain **750** Abbasids control North Africa **789** Independent Idrisid dynasty founded in Morocco **868–905** Tulunid dynasty rules Egypt and Syria **926** Fatimid dynasty conquers Morocco **969** Fatimid dynasty reunites most of North Africa under Arab rule	**700s** Viking raids on western Europe **750** Abbasid dynasty founded in Baghdad **c.850** Collapse of Mayan empire

1001–1415

1054 Berber Almoravid dynasty founded (Western Sahara) **1069** Almoravids conquer Morocco **1147** Berber Almohad dynasty founded (Western Sahara) **1150** Almoravid empire collapses; succeeded by Almohads **1169** Collapse of Fatimid empire **1269** Collapse of Almohad empire **1250** Mamluks rule Egypt **1415** Portuguese capture Ceuta, the first European colony in Africa	**1066** Normans conquer England **c.1200** Inca empire established **c.1200** Aztecs found small states in Mexico **1209** Genghis Khan begins Mongol conquest of Asia **1346–1349** Black Death ravages Europe **1368** Ming dynasty rules China

1416–1700

1505 Funj kingdom founded in Sudan **1517** Ottoman Turks conquer Egypt **1574** Ottomans control all of North Africa except Morocco **c.1600** Darfur established in Sudan **1670** Alawids rule Morocco **1700** Funj kingdom at greatest extent	**1492** Voyage of Columbus **1519–1522** Voyage of Magellan **1600s** French and British set up colonies in North America **1619** First African slaves arrive in Jamestown, Virginia

1701–1900

1798 Napoleon of France conquers Egypt **1801** French ejected from Egypt **1805** Egypt independent **1816** Barbary pirates crushed in Algiers by British and Dutch fleet **1830** France seizes Algiers and extends its rule to spread further inland **1869** Suez Canal opened **1874** Egypt annexes Darfur **1875** Egypt sells its shares in the Suez Canal to Britain **1880s** European powers compete fiercely and divide Africa between them **1881** French rule begins in Tunisia **1882** British rule begins in Egypt **1882** Mahdist revolt begins in Sudan	**c.1750** Industrial Revolution in Britain **1776–1783** US Revolutionary War against British **1789–1799** French Revolution takes place **1804** Napoleon becomes emperor of France **1815** Napoleon defeated at Waterloo **1848** Marx and Engels publish *Communist Manifesto* **1861–1865** US Civil War **1865** US abolishes slavery **1871** Germany united

© DIAGRAM

Colonial occupation and independence

NORTH AFRICAN EVENTS	WORLD EVENTS
1885 Spanish establish colony of Rio de Oro (Western Sahara)	
1898 British crush Mahdist uprising in Sudan	

1901–1945

NORTH AFRICAN EVENTS	WORLD EVENTS
1911 Italy conquers Libya	**1905** First Russian Revolution
1912 French and Spanish take full control over Morocco	**1911** Chinese Revolution establishes a republic
1914–1918 World War I: Egypt used as a British military base	**1917** US enters World War I
1914 Britain makes Egypt a protectorate	**1917** Communists take power in second Russian Revolution
1919–1934 Parts of Egypt and Sudan given to Libya	**1929** Wall Street Crash leads to The Great Depression
1921–1926 Abd el-Krim rebellion in Rif mountains of Morocco	
1922 Britain grants Egypt nominal independence	
1923 Egypt becomes a constitutional monarchy	**1941** US enters World War II after attack on Pearl Harbor
1939–1945 World War II	
1940–1941 British defeat Italian invasion of Egypt	**1945** Dropping of two atomic bombs on Japan ends World War II
1942 British defeat German-Italian army at El Alamein	
1942 US and British troops land in Morocco and conquer northwest Africa	**1945** United Nations established
1945 Arab League formed in Cairo	
1945 Britain and France control Libya	

1946–1962

NORTH AFRICAN EVENTS	WORLD EVENTS
1948 Egypt and other Arab states invade Israel	**1949** North Atlantic Treaty Organization (NATO) set up
1951 Libya gains independence	**1954** French defeated in Vietnam
1952 King Farouk of Egypt deposed in military coup	**1955** Warsaw Pact set up in eastern Europe
1953 Egypt becomes a republic	**1956** USSR crushes Hungarian uprising
1954 Nasser seizes power in Egypt	
1954 Algerian war of independence begins against France	**1957** European Common Market, later the European Union, set up
1955 Civil war starts in Sudan	
1956 Sudan and Tunisia both gain independence	**1957** Ghana becomes first independent Black African nation
1956 French and Spanish Morocco united as independent nation	**1960** Organization of Petroleum Exporting Countries (OPEC) formed
1956 Britain, France, and Israel invade Egypt during Suez crisis	
1961 Libya starts to export oil	
1962 Algeria becomes independent	**1961** Berlin Wall divides Germany

1963–1980

NORTH AFRICAN EVENTS	WORLD EVENTS
1963 Organization of African Unity (OAU) founded	**1963** US president John F Kennedy assassinated
1965 Military coup in Algeria led by Boumedienne	**1965–1973** US troops in Vietnam
1967 Six-Day War between Egypt with its Arab allies and Israel	
1969 Monarchy overthrown in Libya; Colonel Quaddafi takes power	**1969** Neil Armstrong is first person to land on the moon
1970 Nasser dies; succeeded by Anwar Sadat	**1973** Worldwide oil crisis owing to the Yom Kippur War
1972 End of first Sudanese civil war	
1973 Yom Kippur War between Egypt and Israel	**1974** Revolution in Portugal leads to its withdrawal from its African colonies
1975 Western Sahara ceded by Spain to Morocco and Mauritania	
1976 Morocco and Mauritania occupy Western Sahara	**1979** Islamic fundamentalists take power in Iran

NORTH AFRICAN EVENTS		WORLD EVENTS

NORTH AFRICAN EVENTS

1979 Camp David talks end state of war between Egypt and Israel

1981–2002

1981 Sadat assassinated; succeeded by Hosni Mubarak

1983 Sudan adopts *sharia* (Islamic law); civil war breaks out again

1984 First free elections in Egypt

1985 OAU admits Western Sahara representatives; Morocco leaves organization

1986 US bombs Tripoli, Libya

1988 Civil unrest increases in Algeria

1988 Libya suspected of bombing Pan Am aircraft, which crashes over Scotland

1989 Military coup in Sudan

1990 Massive famine in Sudan kills thousands

1991 Islamic party banned in Algeria after winning elections

1992 Islamic terror campaign begins in Algeria

1992 UN imposes sanctions on Libya for refusing to hand over suspected terrorists

1993 Islamic militants kill tourists in Egypt

2000 Amnesty leads to relative peace in Algeria

2001 One of the two Libyans suspected of 1988 Pan Am bombing found guilty

WORLD EVENTS

1979 USSR invades Afghanistan

1980–1988 Iran-Iraq War

1982–1985 Israel invades Lebanon

1986 Chernobyl nuclear accident in USSR

1989 Tiannanmen Square massacre in China

1990-1991 Gulf War after Iraq invades Kuwait

1990–1991 Communism collapses in E. Europe and USSR

1991–1995 War in Yugoslavia

1993 Israeli-Palestinian agreement

1994 Multiparty elections in South Africa end apartheid

2001 Terrorist attack on World Trade Center in New York leads to invasion of Afghanistan

2002 A six-month ceasefire in Sudan leads to successful peace talks ending the civil war

COLONIAL OCCUPATION AND INDEPENDENCE

Country	Independence	Occupied *	Colonial powers
Algeria	Jul 3, 1962	1842	France
Egypt	Feb 28, 1922	1798–1801 1882	France Britain
Libya	Dec 24, 1951	1911	Italy
Morocco: (French) (Spanish)	Mar 2, 1956 Apr 7, 1956	1912 1912	France Spain
Sudan	Jan 1, 1956	1898	Under joint British and Egyptian rule
Tunisia	Mar 20, 1956	1881	France
Western Sahara (as *Río de Oro*)	(ceded to Morocco and Mauritania in 1975)	1885	Spain

* The years given for the beginning of occupation by the modern-day nations are those by which a significant area of coastal and hinterland territory had been occupied by a colonial power.

Moroccan flag, map and dove
A 1966 stamp marks the tenth anniversary of independence.

Independence Day in Sudan
A stamp, issued in 1956, marks this momentous occasion.

© DIAGRAM

PREHISTORY TO THE IRON AGE

Early farming
This reaping knife (below), found in Algeria, was probably used for harvesting cereal crops, such as millet (above left) and sorghum (above right) and wild grasses.

The origin of humankind is still a closely-argued question. Until recently, most palaeontologists agreed that the earliest pre-human genus – Australopithecus – flourished in the Rift Valley of East Africa about 4 million years ago. In 2002, however, apparently 7-million year-old humanoid remains were discovered in Chad. Whatever the final verdict, it can at least be said that by about 2.5 million years ago, a recognizable human ancestor, *Homo habilis*, had evolved in East Africa. These early hominids made cutting and carving tools from pieces of stone they had worked into shape.

The Stone Age

A major advance came abut 1.8 million years ago, when the bigger-brained *Homo erectus* replaced the primitive *Homo habilis*. *Homo erectus* used stones to make hand-axes and cleavers to chop down trees and also to cut up the carcasses of animals they had killed. By about 120,000 years ago, *Homo erectus* had evolved into a successful hunter-gatherer. Members of the species lived by hunting wild animals and gathering edible berries and fruits. They had developed a simple but effective technology in wood and stone to make weapons and other items and, above all, had discovered how to use fire, which was important not just in increasing their range of edible foods but in making tools and in warding off predators. Remains of *Homo erectus* have been found throughout the Sahara, the Nile Valley, and in the Atlas Mountains of northwest Africa.

The next important period in human development occurred about 100,000 years ago, when *Homo sapiens sapiens* – the first modern humans – emerged in southern Africa. By about 35,000 years ago, these early people had

Hunting hippos (above)
This drawing, from the time when there were many rivers and lakes in the Sahara, shows a hunter in a canoe in search of a hippopotamus.

spread throughout Africa, as remains in the Nile Valley and along the north coast indicate. The Ice Age, which lasted from 20,000–10,000 BCE, turned Africa into a dry, hot continent, but as the ice sheets in Europe retreated north, the Sahara and other parts of North Africa became wetter and more fertile. This allowed more people to settle in the region, where they domesticated cattle, sheep, and goats, grew sorghum, millet, and barley, and began to live a more settled, pastoral lifestyle. These early farmers also invented sophisticated tools, such as grindstones to make flour, made pottery, and developed a wide range of other technical skills.

A gallery in the rocks (above)
Most of the Saharan rock paintings were found at Tassili-n-Ajjer, a block of sandstone weathered by wind and water, situated on the Algerian/Libyan border.

Taming giraffes (left)
Painted between 6000–4000 BCE, the artist illustrates one of the many attempts made at this time to tame species, such as the giraffe, in the Sahara.

Historical events

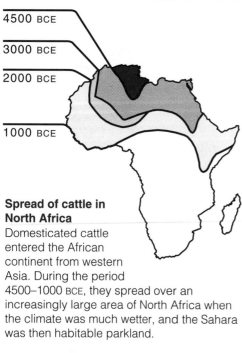

4500 BCE
3000 BCE
2000 BCE
1000 BCE

Spread of cattle in North Africa
Domesticated cattle entered the African continent from western Asia. During the period 4500–1000 BCE, they spread over an increasingly large area of North Africa when the climate was much wetter, and the Sahara was then habitable parkland.

The first civilizations

The first settled farming villages appeared in the Nile Valley by 4500 BCE. Over the next 1,200 years, these villages grew in size and sophistication, as villagers developed a range of new skills, most notably the ability to heat and cast copper to make tools, jewelry, and other items. Later, they began to mix the copper with tin to make the alloy bronze, a far harder material with many more practical uses. The development and use of this technology allowed these villages to create advanced civilizations. They worked copper and bronze for both practical and ornamental uses, made slate palettes and stone maceheads to grind cosmetics, and became skilled craftworkers. Expeditions set out to mine and quarry copper, tin, gold, and turquoise up the Nile as far south as Nubia and east out of Egypt into the Sinai peninsula.

A pastoral way of life (right)
Herds of cattle and flocks of sheep and goats feature strongly in rock paintings found at Tassili-n-Ajjer, Algeria (6000–1200 BCE). Most of its inhabitants were pastoral people who herded cattle and other animals for a living.

The people who lived alongside the River Nile had one huge advantage over their neighbors elsewhere in North Africa. Every year, the Nile flooded, covering its floodplains with layers of fertile mud. As the floods receded, crops could be planted in the fertile soil and then irrigated with water drawn from the river. With a plentiful supply of both food and water, the Egyptians were able to develop a settled lifestyle. By c.3300 BCE, the first walled towns were built at Naqada and Hierakonopolis in Upper Egypt.

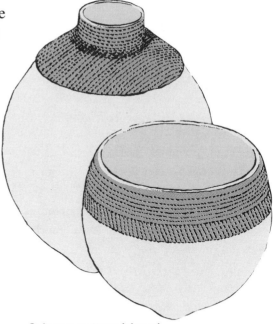

Saharan pottery (above)
Making pottery was just one of many skills developed by the farming villagers from the Saharan Atlas and northwest Sahara from 4500 BCE onwards.

The end of an era (left)
A contemporary rock painting depicts an invading charioteer from the north; the pastoral people were driven south from Tassili-n-Ajjer from around 1200 BCE.

Early civilizations in Africa	
c.4.4 mya	*Australopithecus ramidus* evolves in East Africa
c.2 mya	*Homo habilis* evolves in East Africa
c.1.6 mya	*Homo erectus* replaces *Homo habilis*
c.400,000 BCE	*Homo sapiens sapiens* emerges in southern Africa
c.35,000	*Home sapiens sapiens* settles in whole of Africa
c.20,000–10,000	Ice Age turns North Africa dry and hot
c.8500	First people settle the Sahara
c.7000	First pottery made in the Sahara
c.6500	Cattle domesticated in the Sahara
c.6000	Rock art created in the Sahara
c.4500	Settled villages emerge in Nile Valley
c.4000	Sahara begins to dry out
c.3500	Ancient Egyptians develop copper and later bronzemaking skills
c.3300	First walled towns built in Egypt

© DIAGRAM

Life in the Sahara

Sahara means desert in Arabic, but the vast, hot, and dry place we know today was not always a desert. About 10,500 years ago – after the end of the last Ice Age – the Sahara was green and fertile, with grassy plains, broad lakes, flowing rivers and a cooler, wetter climate. Many people lived in the Sahara, and left a record of their life in a series of remarkable paintings on the rocks of Tassili-n-Ajjer, southern Algeria, and elsewhere. Tassili-n-Ajjer is a high plateau – up to 7,400 ft (2,426 m) above sea level – eroded over the centuries by wind and water into a maze of pillar-like columns of rock separated by deep gorges and canyons.

Today Tassili-n-Ajjer is intensely hot during the day and bitterly cold at night, but 10,000 years ago its climate and landscape were very different, as the name of the place – "plateau of the rivers" – indicates. The remains of a fossilized forest on its barren slopes show that it was once heavily wooded. Elephants, giraffes, and other animals roamed the area, as did hippopotami, the bones of which have been found by archaeologists in a dry riverbed south of the area. Crocodiles and fish swam in the rivers, and the entire area teemed with wildlife.

A different view: the Sahara 10,000 years ago
After the end of the Ice Age the Sahara was vastly different from the desert we know today. People lived a pastoral existence, raising domesticated livestock and hunted wild animals on the grassy plains and wooded slopes in the cool, wet climate of the time.

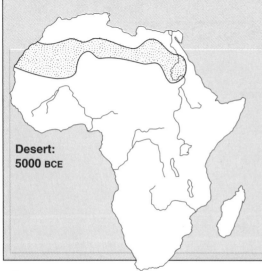

**Desert:
5000 BCE**

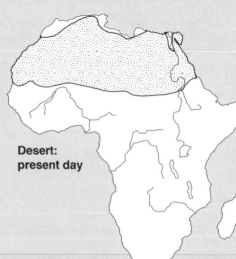

**Desert:
present day**

Extent of the Sahara
The map (far left) shows the approximate area occupied by the Sahara c.5000 BCE; the map (left) defines the limit of the desert today.

We know so much about Tassili-n-Ajjer because of the paintings, which were executed in a few bright colors, mostly yellow, red, and brown, obtained from reddish brown or yellow ocher, which is a type of clay. The paintings are mostly found at the bottom of the gullies on the sides of the sandstone columns. Many of the images are placed on top of earlier ones, some up to a dozen layers thick. This would suggest that the artists regarded certain sites as sacred and created new paintings on top of old ones to placate their gods.

The earliest paintings date from c. 6000 BCE and show stylized human figures wearing flared leggings and performing some strange dance or ritual. Later paintings, from c. 5000 BCE, show herds of cattle, flocks of wild sheep and goats, giraffes, the now extinct giant buffalo, and other animals. Paintings of horse-drawn chariots date from about 1200 BCE, while those showing camels probably date to about 100 BCE. In some, the local people are shown herding cattle and other animals, while one shows a hunter in a canoe pursuing a hippopotamus. From these images, we know that the local people were pastoralists who raised domesticated livestock as well as hunting wild animals. They used boats to cross the many rivers and lakes, and had bows, arrows, and other weapons with which to kill their game. The appearance of chariots suggests that invaders from the north moved into the area in about 1200 BCE, eventually driving the pastoralists south into the Sahel. By then, climate changes in the area were raising the temperature and reducing the rainfall, gradually transforming the Sahara into the hot, dry desert we know today.

KINGDOMS OF THE NILE

Along the banks of the River Nile, two remarkable civilizations emerged at the end of the 4th millennium. One of them, Nubia, is the oldest known civilization in black Africa. The other, Egypt, was one of the most enduring civilizations in world history.

Ancient kingdom of Nubia
The historical region of Nubia covered parts of present-day southern Egypt and northern Sudan, extending southward up the Nile from its first cataract (a rock-strewn stretch of river making navigation impossible) south of Aswan almost as far as present-day Khartoum, capital of Sudan. Kush, the first Nubian kingdom, emerged in around 3200 BCE and expanded considerably from 2400 BCE, reaching its greatest extent in 1750 BCE – when it stretched up beyond the fourth cataract – until it was conquered in 1500 CE by the Egyptians, who had always regarded Nubia as theirs by right. Tombs and temple remains show that the Nubians were builders of great style and ingenuity, although they borrowed heavily from neighboring Egypt. They were also skilled potters and great traders, shipping precious goods such as spices, ivory, ebony, and ostrich feathers, as well as African slaves, from East Africa down the Nile to Egypt. Stones, gems, and precious metals mined in the desert were also transported north.

Greatest extent
The kingdom of Nubia was at its greatest geographical extent c.1750 BCE.

Ancient kingdom of Egypt
The first villages were built in Egypt about 4500 BCE, with walled towns appearing c.3300, but it was not until c.3050 that these were united under a single king known as a pharaoh. From 2920, a series of dynasties (ruling families) ran the country until, in c.1640, the "Hyksos," literally "rulers of foreign lands," or "foreigners," took control. After they were expelled by Thebans from the south of Egypt in 1532, the New Kingdom of pharaohs rapidly built up its power until, during the reign of Tuthmosis I (1504–1492) it dominated the entire Middle East, stretching as far as present-day Syria. Egypt remained a major regional power until it began to decline after the end of the 20th dynasty in 1070 BCE.

Greatest extent
The kingdom of Egypt was at its greatest geographical extent c.1500 BCE.

ing Narmer and Horus, the god
he decoration on this vase commemorates
he triumph of Narmer over his enemies.
Horus appears as a falcon (top right).

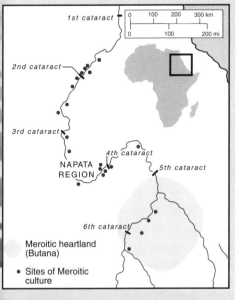

Greatest extent
The Meroitic kingdom was at its greatest
geographical extent c.150 CE.

The kingdom of Egypt	
c.3050 BCE	Foundation of kingdom of Egypt
Early Dynastic Period	
2920–2770	1st dynasty
2770–2649	2nd dynasty
Old Kingdom	
2649–2575	3rd dynasty
2575–2465	4th dynasty
2465–2323	5th dynasty
2323–2150	6th dynasty
2150–2134	7th–8th dynasties
First Intermediate Period	
2134–2040	9th–10th dynasties
2134–2040	11th dynasty
Middle Kingdom	
2040–1991	11th dynasty – all Egypt
1991–1783	12th dynasty
1783–c.1640	13th dynasty
	14th dynasty: group of minor kings contemporary with 13th dynasty
Second Intermediate Period	
c.1640–1532	15th dynasty – Hyksos rule
	16th dynasty: group of minor kings contemporary with 15th dynasty
c.1640–1550	17th dynasty – Theban
New Kingdom	
1550–1307	18th dynasty
1307–1196	19th dynasty
1196–1070	20th dynasty
Late Dynastic Period	
1070–945	21st dynasty
945–712	22nd dynasty
828–712	23rd dynasty
724–712	24th dynasty
770–712	25th dynasty – Nubia and Thebes
712–657	25th dynasty – Nubia and all of Egypt
664–525	26th dynasty
525–404	27th dynasty – Persian rule
404–399	28th dynasty
399–380	29th dynasty
380–343	30th dynasty
343–332	31st dynasty – 2nd period of Persian rule
Greco-Roman Period	
332–304	Macedonian period
304–30	Ptolemaic period
30 BCE–395 CE	Roman emperors
395–640	Byzantine period

Gods and rulers

The Egyptians worshipped numerous gods, many of which were represented by animals. Confusingly, the same animal could represent two different gods in different places, while each of the 42 different "nomes," or administrative districts, had its own god.

The main Egyptian god was the sun-god Re, who took the form of Khepri, the scarab beetle who rolled the sun disc above the eastern horizon at dawn. During the day, he was Re-Harakhty, the great hawk flying high in the sky. Re was responsible for everything in creation, from people and animals to the fertility of the soil, as well as for the pharaoh's journey through creation. The people of Thebes worshipped a sun god called Amun, and so over time Amun became identified with Re and was known as Amun-Re, who became king of the gods and protected the pharaoh when he went on military campaigns. Pharaoh Akhenaten (reigned 1353–1335) saw the sun god Aton as a disc with rays ending in human hands which held the sign of life to the royal family. He banished all other gods and created the world's first monotheistic state, but his son Tutankhamun restored the full pantheon of gods during his short reign (1333–1323).

Other important gods included the creator-god Ptah and the fertility goddess Isis, wife and sister of Osiris, judge of the dead and god of the afterlife, and mother of Horus, the sky-god. The pharaohs were believed to be incarnations of Horus.

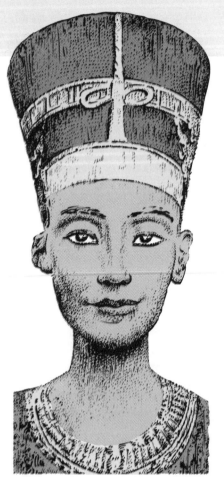

Nefertiti
An Egyptian queen of the 14th century BCE, she was instrumental in changing Egyptian religion from the worship of many gods to that of only one – Aton, the sun disk.

Temples

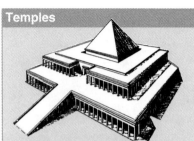

Temple of Mentuhetep
Constructed in 2065 BCE at Der el-Bahari in Thebes, this temple is a typical example of the architecture of the Middle Kingdom.

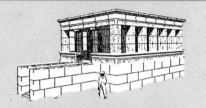

Temple, Island of Elephantine
This is an example of one of the Mammisi temples, which stood within the enclosures of larger temples. Located near present-day Aswan, it was constructed in 1408 BCE.

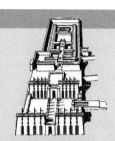

Great temple of Amun
Often considered to be the grandest of all Egyptian temples, this building owes its impressive scale to the work of many pharaohs. It was constructed between 1530–323 BCE.

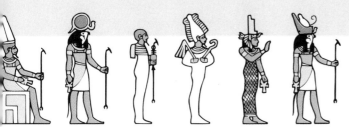

Amon-Re   Re   Ptah   Osiris   Isis   Horus

Ancient Egyptian gods
Some of these figures are portrayed with animal heads on human bodies, reflecting the contrasting natures of the deities.

The Egyptians built vast temples in which to worship their gods. The pharaoh was supposed to carry out the duties of the high priest in every temple in Egypt, but the chief priest usually took his place. The office of chief priest often ran in a single family for generations, and the priesthood itself had great wealth and power. Titles such as God's Servant indicate their status. Apart from conducting services on a rota system, priests maintained temple property and kept administrative records. A select few were involved in ceremonies in the temple's inner shrine, which housed a golden statue of the temple's god. Here the priest would decorate the statue and make an offering of food before leaving the sanctuary as someone swept the floor after him so not to leave any traces of his presence behind.

The Egyptian royal family
Tutankhamun, an Egyptian pharaoh of the 18th dynasty, is here depicted with his wife who was also his sister.

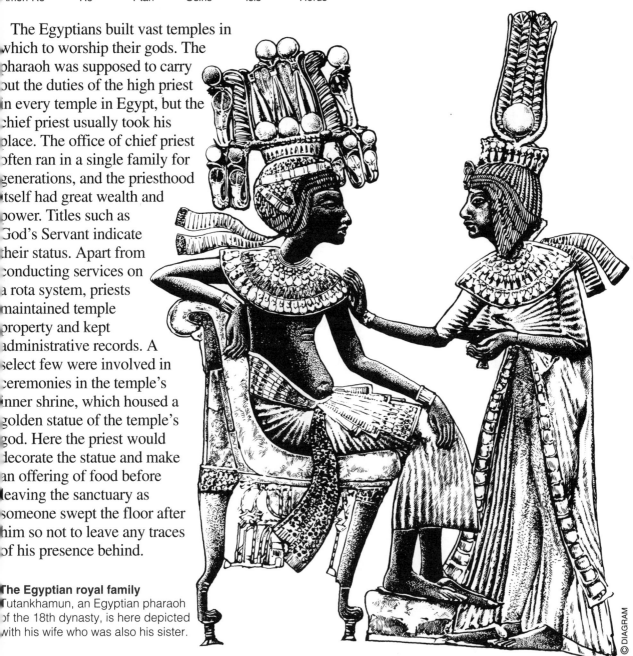

© DIAGRAM

Life in Ancient Egypt

Egyptian society was divided into three main classes: upper, middle, and lower. The upper class comprised the royal family, religious and government officials, army officers, doctors, and wealthy landowners. Merchants, manufacturers, and skilled artisans and workers, such as architects, engineers, teachers, scribes, accountants, stonemasons, and carpenters, made up the middle class. The vast majority of people, however, were lower class laborers and their families who mostly worked on farms owned by the upper classes. The main crops were wheat and barley, which were often given in place of wages to the workers. Vegetables and fruit were also grown. The staple food was bread made from wheat; the main drink was beer made from barley. Flax was grown to make linen, and cattle, sheep, donkeys, and pigs were raised.

Bringing in the catch
The use of small nets was a popular method of fishing in contrast to submerging baskets, spearing, or angling.

A typical trader
Trading vessels were often fitted with special equipment to facilitate the loading and unloading of bulky cargo.

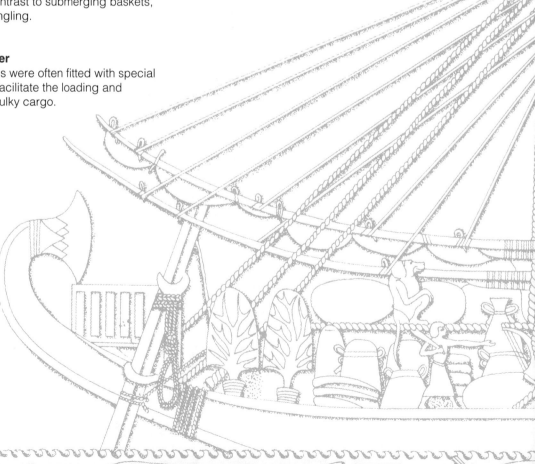

Gathering the harvest
This illustration shows lower-class laborers cutting down the wheat in the fields at harvest time.

Going to market
A herder is shown counting cattle in this tomb wall painting.

© DIAGRAM

The afterlife

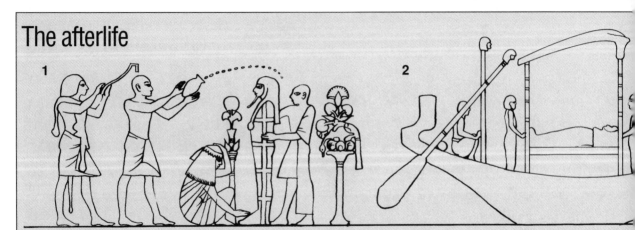

1

2

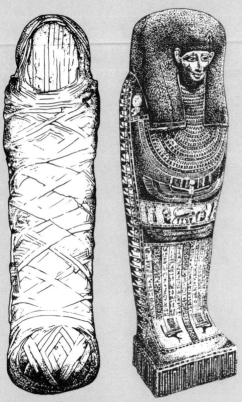

Preserving the dead

The ancient Egyptians believed in an afterlife in which people could again use their own bodies. Once a person died, their internal organs were removed, empty cavities were filled, the body was embalmed with fluid, and finally it was wrapped in linen bandages. The mummified form (above left) was then placed in a wooden or stone coffin (above right). If the deceased were wealthy or royal, then the coffin would be elaborately decorated.

Pharaohs, noblemen, and state officials were buried inside vast stone pyramids. The first pyramid – the so-called Step Pyramid because it rose in six steps – was built by the architect Imhotep for King Djoser i c.2630 BCE. It represented a gigantic stairway for the king to climb up to join the sun-god in the sky. Few step pyramids were built, for in the reign of King Sneferu (2575–2551 BCE) a new style of pyramid was built with sloping sides. These true pyramids recreated the mound that had emerged out of the watery wilderness at the beginning of time, or which the sun-god stood and brought the other gods into existence.

The largest pyramid of all was built at Giza, outside modern-day Cairo, for King Khufu (Cheops) c.2528 BCE. This vast edifice was 450 ft (146 m) tall, contained more than 2.3 million blocks of limestone, and probably took about 20 years to build. Inside, a sloping gallery led to the king's chamber at the heart of the pyramid, where his sarcophagus was placed.

In all, about 40 pyramids were built in Egypt until, in c.2150 BCE, the pharaohs chose to be buried in tombs. A highly visible pyramid attracted grave robbers, so royal tombs were increasingly built in secret underground locations, most notably the Valley of the Kings, a remote valley in the hills across the Nile from Thebes, at one time the capital city of Ancient Egypt. This was the final resting

lace for most pharaohs from Tuthmosis I (reigned 504–1492 BCE) to Ramesses XI (1100–1070 CE). As with the pyramids, all the tombs were built n the west bank of the River Nile, towards the tting sun.

Most royal tombs consisted of a corridor burrowing ep into the hillside; near its entrance was a deep ell or shaft designed both to collect rainwater and ap unwary tomb robbers. At the end of a corridor as the "Hall of Gold," where the king was laid rrounded by furniture, clothing, jewelry, and royal galia for the afterlife. As with the pyramids, the ntents of these tombs were all removed by grave bbers in the centuries that followed burial. The xception was Tutankhamun's tomb, which lay ndiscovered after his death in 1323 BCE until the rchaeologists Lord Caernarvon and Howard Carter umbled upon it in 1922 CE.

Into the afterlife

There were four main stages in reaching the life beyond death:

1 Priests and family performed a ceremony known as "The Opening of the Mouth" which, it was believed, would give the dead person the ability to breathe in the afterlife.

2 Two female mourners, who represented Isis and Nephrhys mourning the death of Osiris, accompanied the mummified corpse which was placed under a canopy.

3 The heart of the deceased was weighed against a feather, the symbol of truth, while Ammit, the "Devourer of the Dead," stood at the ready.

4 Osiris, flanked by other gods, sat in judgement as the balance was presented to him for his verdict.

Writing

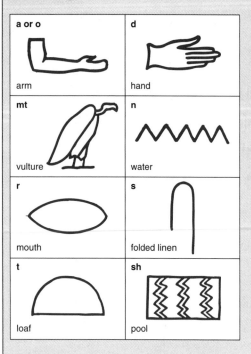

a or o	d
arm	hand
mt	n
vulture	water
r	s
mouth	folded linen
t	sh
loaf	pool

About 3000 BCE, the Egyptians developed a form of writing known as hieroglyphs. The word hieroglyph means "sacred carving" in Greek, because it was used in temples, tombs, and other state monuments, and on official or religious documents.

Hieroglyphs look like a simple picture language because they include birds, animals, body parts, such as an arm or a hand, and everyday items. But, over the years, hieroglyphs developed into a complex writing system whereby a single hieroglyph stood for a whole word or just a single sound. This made some hieroglyphs similar to individual letters of an alphabet. Names of a king or queen were always shown by a group of hieroglyphs enclosed in an oval border known as a cartouche.

Hieroglyphic writing

The ancient Egyptians used picture symbols, called hieroglyphs, to represent sounds and ideas. There were over 700 of them.

Recognizing a pharoah

The name was usually enclosed within an oval border, or cartouche. Symbols which clearly showed the king's (or queen's) titles were set either above or beside them.

Cheops (or Khufu), who built the Great Pyramid at Giza.

Akhenaten, who introduced the worship of a single god. After his death priests tried to eradicate his memory and defaced any carvings bearing his name and portrait.

Tutankhamun, whose mummy and tomb treasure were discovered by Howard Carter.

Ramesses II, whose statues front the great rock temple of Abu Simbel.

Alexander the Great, whose empire stretched from Greece to India.

Cleopatra, the mistress Julius Caes and Mark Antony.

Professional scribes

In total, there were more than 700 different hieroglyphs, which could be written from left to right, right to left, or top to bottom. Highly trained, professional scribes – who held an important position in society, for which they were rewarded with special privileges – were employed just to write hieroglyphs. At first, they carved the signs onto stone or etched them into metal, and used thin reed brushes to write on papyrus scrolls, or thicker brushes made from papyrus twine to write on temple walls or statues. The ink was made by mixing soot and water. Later, they used reed pens, an invention brought to Egypt by the Greeks in 332 BCE.

Practicing his art
A pen, water pot, and palette are shown (above left), and a scribe (above right).

Hieroglyphs to Coptic

Writing hieroglyphs was a time-consuming process. Scribes therefore developed a faster system known as hieratic, which they used for letters, business contracts, and other less important documents.

The complex birds, animals, and objects of hieroglyphics were simplified into more abstract shapes, which were written in a flowing script from right to left. By 600 BCE, *an even simpler and faster script, known as demotic, was developed for use in legal documents. After the Macedonian invasion of 332* BCE, *scribes learned to write Greek, and by 300* CE, *the use of hieroglyphs had completely died out in favour of the Coptic script, based on Greek.*

Meroitic writing
This form of writing, featuring both characters and picture symbols, was used for royal or religious inscriptions.

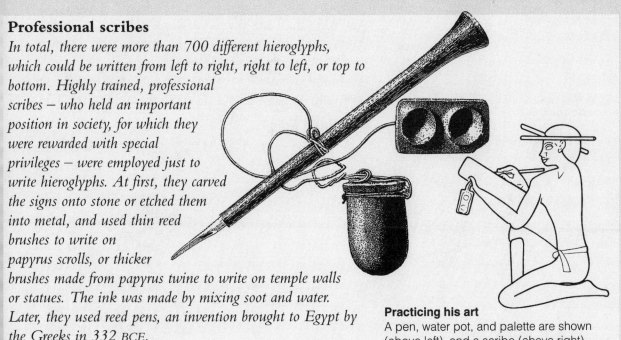

A	B	D	E	Ê	H (KH)
H (KH)	I	K	L	M	N
Ñ	P	Q	R	S	Š (SH)
T	TE	TÊ	W	Y	

© DIAGRAM

EGYPT IN CONFLICT

For more than 1,000 years – from 1070 BCE to the start of Roman rule in 30 BCE – Egypt went through a turbulent period of internal strife, invasion, foreign rule, and gradual decline after its lengthly period of greatness. To its south, Nubia was not immune from these troubles.

A divided Egypt

At the start of the 21st dynasty, in 1070 BCE, Egypt was effectively two countries: one in the north

A sea of troubles
Many wall friezes of the time depicted both the internal strife within Egypt itself, and conflicts on foreign soil in its attempt to extend its empire overseas.

ruled by the pharaohs from their new capital of Tanis, in the Nile Delta, and one in the south ruled by the high priests at Thebes. Shoshenq I (reigned 945–924), the first pharaoh of the 22nd dynasty, reunited the country and extended Egyptian control northeast into Palestine and rebuilt trading relationships with Phoenicia, in what is now Lebanon.

Meanwhile, an independent kingdom of Nubia flourished from its capital at Napata. This period of peace and prosperity lasted for a century until the reign of Takelot II (860–835), when conflicts about who was to become high priest led to civil war in Egypt. Rival dynasties jostled for power so that by 724, there were four dynasties ruling different parts of Egypt at the same time. One of these – the 25th dynasty – was started by a Nubian king, Kashta, who seized control of Egypt as far north as Thebes in 770. His successor, Piankhy (750–712), eventually conquered the whole of Egypt by the end of his reign.

A ceremonial war-ax
Made of bronze and gold, the blade depicts an Egyptian king defeating an enemy.

© DIAGRAM

Brothers in arms
The Assyrian infantry consisted of "files;" each file was made up of a spearman with a shield, and an archer.

Kushite invaders
This statue features Narwa, the governor of Thebes, during a period of Kushite occupation of Egypt in the 7th and 8th centuries BCE. The Kushites were eventually expelled from Egypt by the Assyrians.

Foreign control

Nubian control of Egypt produced half a century of peace and prosperity. Under Shabaka (712–698) and his successors, the Nubian pharaohs re-established the capital at Memphis in the north of the country, put down rival claimants to the throne, and presided over a period of economic growth and considerable artistic activity. For example, new buildings and temples were constructed and old ones were restored.

The only rival to Nubian-run Egypt was Assyria, a major Middle Eastern empire based in the Tigris and Euphrates river valleys in what is now Iraq. Between the two lay the states of Palestine, which looked to Egypt for support against the Assyrian threats to their independence. At first Egypt declined to help, but in 701 an Egyptian force fought for the small state of Judah against the Assyrian king Sennacherib (704–681). The battle was inconclusive, but in 674 the Assyrians tried to invade Egypt. That attack was defeated, but in 671 the Assyrians captured the Egyptian capital of Memphis, driving out its Nubian rulers. Further attacks in 667 and 663–657 led to a period of Assyrian rule over the whole of Egypt through local puppet rulers until Psammetichus I (reigned 664–610) re-established control and forced the Assyrians out by 653. To do this, he had to employ mercenaries from Greece and Caria (modern-day southwest Turkey), thus introducing a group of foreigners into the country whose specialization in warfare and trade gave them a disproportionate influence in Egypt's affairs. The lengthy period of Egyptian isolation from events and empires elsewhere in the world had now come to an end.

For the next century, Egypt tried to rebuild its economy and pursued a sensible policy of trying to balance power on its northeast border by supporting the rivals of whichever country was dominant in the region. Thus Egypt supported Lydia (western Turkey) and Babylon against Assyria, and then changed sides to support Assyria against the new Babylonian empire of Nebuchadnezzar II (604–562) and then the growing power of Persia. Fleets of war triremes were equipped in both the Red and Mediterranean Seas, and an attempt was made to build a canal between the Nile and the Red Sea.

Persian control

This juggling act eventually failed in 525 BCE, when the Persians under Cambyses invaded the country and set up the 27th dynasty. For more than a century, Egypt was merely a distant province of Persia, whose main interests lay elsewhere. The Persians introduced the camel – of major importance to the future of the country – and completed the Nile-Red Sea canal. Egyptian resistance to Persian rule began around 490 BCE, but it was not until 404 BCE that the Persians were finally thrown out of Egypt. Further Persian invasions in 373 and 350 were repulsed, but in 343 the Persians again invaded and conquered the country.

This time, their rule was short-lived, for in 333 BCE Alexander the Great of Macedon, in northern Greece, swept through the Middle East and in 332, without a struggle, he took control of Egypt, where he was welcomed as a liberator from Persian rule. He planned to build a new city on the coast, called Alexandria, but his reign was brief, for in 323, he died in Babylon, aged 33.

Meroitic Sudan

In the upheavals caused by the Assyrian invasions in the years after 674, Nubia lost control of Egypt by 657 and became an entirely separate kingdom once again. It successfully fought off an Egyptian invasion in 591, but rapidly declined to a shadow of its former power.

In c.300 BCE, the Nubian capital moved south from Napata up the Nile to Meroe, close to the sixth cataract. Here a powerful new Meroitic kingdom emerged. The town became an important center of ironmaking, producing exports to Egypt and wealth for Nubia itself. Extravagant tombs and temples were built in and around Meroe, and the people developed their own alphabetical script. This prosperous and creative civilization flourished independently of Egypt for more than six centuries, until the Ethiopian kingdom of Axum conquered it in 324 CE.

A colossus from the Temple of Isis
The Meroitic kingdom flourished on the Nile for more than six centuries, and left behind its own unique artistic legacy.

A crown from a tomb at Ballana
Ancient reliefs found in the Sudan depict crowns similar to those worn by Meroitic royalty over 2,000 years ago in Egypt.

© DIAGRAM

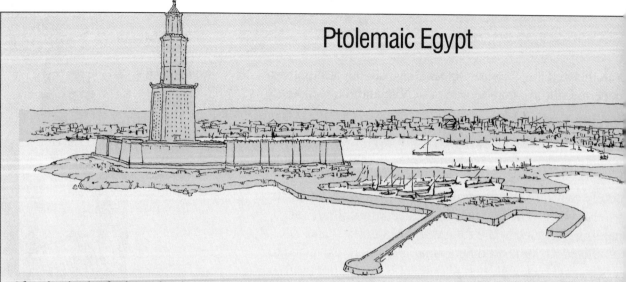

Ptolemaic Egypt

After the death of Alexander the Great in 323 BCE, two short-lived successors ruled Egypt until in 304, Ptolemy – one of Alexander's generals and, after his death, satrap or provincial governor of Egypt – proclaimed himself king. The Ptolemaic dynasty ruled Egypt for almost 300

Alexander the Great
Welcomed in Egypt as a liberator from Persian rule, he planned the foundation of Alexandria, the most important city in the Greek world.

Ptolemaic Egypt

304 BCE Ptolemy proclaims himself king of Egypt and establishes Ptolemaic dynasty. During his reign he builds the library and museum at Alexandria

284 Ptolemy succeeded by Ptolemy II, who reigns until 246; the lighthouse at Pharos is completed

205 Ptolemaic Empire reaches its greatest extent

168 Syrians invade Egypt and briefly seize control

51 Cleopatra VII becomes co-ruler with Ptolemy XIII

31 Cleopatra and Mark Antony defeated at Actium

30 Cleopatra commits suicide; Egypt absorbed into Roman Empire

years. The Ptolemies were Greeks but ruled Egypt as a separate country and, despite their sometimes oppressive rule, did put the interests of Egypt first.

The first four Ptolemies – who reigned until 205 – were strong rulers. They annexed Palestine and pushed the border south towards Nubia and west into Libya. For a time, the Mediterranean island of Cyprus, parts of Anatolia (modern-day Turkey) and a large part of the eastern Aegean Sea and its many islands were controlled by Egypt. Above all, they continued with the construction of Alexandria, as planned by Alexander the Great, and turned it into the most important city in the Greek world, building a massive library and museum. However, Egypt had to struggle for control of the eastern Mediterranean and Palestine with the powerful Seleucid Empire of Persia, and was briefly invaded and conquered by Antiochus IV Epiphanes of Syria, who proclaimed himself king in 168 BCE.

At home, the Ptolemaic dynasty did much to reform the national infrastructure. They ran state monopolies of corn, oil-producing crops, mining, and salt, and owned all the land – other than that controlled by the temples – which they rented out to local people. They also organized national and local registers to record all the people, houses, and animals for tax purposes, and set up the most advanced

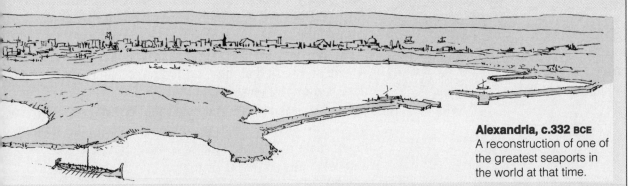

Alexandria, c.332 BCE
A reconstruction of one of the greatest seaports in the world at that time.

system of banking in the world at that time. Above all, they promoted the planting and harvesting of two crops per year, rather than the usual one.

All these measures did much to enrich the government and ensure that the dynasty retained a strong grip on the Egyptian people. As a result, the Ptolemies often faced considerable unrest and rebellion, particularly in the south of the country, and were often undermined by conspiracies within the ruling family.

The Ptolemies supported the Egyptian religion and built many new temples. Animal worship grew in popularity among both Egyptians and Greeks, and whole mortuary towns were built for the mummification and worship of animals, particularly cats, which were often consulted as oracles. The Greek language became widely spoken and for official and public pronouncements was often written alongside hieroglyphics and demotic Egyptian, most famously on the Rosetta Stone.

Despite their many successes, the Ptolemies were unable to withstand the growing power of the Roman Empire. In 51 BCE Cleopatra VII became co-ruler of Egypt alongside Ptolemy XIII but was driven out in 48. She was restored to her throne by the Roman dictator Julius Caesar and, in 47, bore a son she said was his. In 46 she and her child went to Rome with Caesar, but returned to Egypt after his assassination in 44. Three years later she met the Roman general Mark Antony; in due course she bore him twin children and pledged Egypt's support for his campaign against Octavian to control the Roman state. As a result, Egypt became caught up in the struggle for supremacy inside the Roman Empire. Octavian declared war on both Mark Antony and Cleopatra and defeated them at the Battle of Actium in 31. A year later, Cleopatra committed suicide, and Egypt became part of the Roman Empire.

Cleopatra
She was the last, and the most famous, of the Ptolemaic dynasty, and ruled Egypt before it became part of the Roman Empire. Her ambition was to restore the dynasty's power to the heights it had once reached under Ptolemy II.

© DIAGRAM

BERBERS AND PHOENICIANS

A Carthaginian coin

Carthage had its own currency from c.400 BCE. An African elephant, similar to one used by Hannibal during the Second Punic War (218–201 BCE) appears on this coin.

While the Egyptians established their civilization in the Nile Valley, other peoples were settling along the coast of North Africa and developing their own civilizations, notably the Berbers, Phoenicians, and Greeks.

The Berbers are the earliest known inhabitants of North Africa and settled along the Mediterranean coast by 3000 BCE. Although there is little historical knowledge of their existence, it is known that by about 650 BCE, the whole of the North African coast, from the Atlantic in the west to the borders of Egypt in the east, was under Berber control. They shared their region, however, with a number of powerful states, notably Carthage.

Carthage

According to legend, the city-state of Carthage, near present-day Tunis, was founded in 814 BCE by Dido, daughter of the king of Tyre, after her brother murdered her husband and she fled her home with just a small group of warriors. Dido asked the Berber inhabitants of the area for a plot of land on which to build a city and was offered as much as could be surrounded by a bull's hide. She chose the largest bull and ordered its hide to be cut into thin strips, which laid end to end surrounded a large piece of land. Archaeological remains of the city, however, suggest that Carthage was founded at least 100 years later than this story would suggest.

What is true, however, is that Carthage was one of the many colonies established by Phoenician seafarers from

Carthage in all its glory

The illustration below is a reconstruction of the city before its destruction at the hands of the Romans. The view looks out from the Citadel towards the two excellent harbors: the outer area was used by merchant shipping, whereas the inner one housed warships. Surrounded on three sides by the sea, the city's fourth side comprised a huge defensive wall against aggressors.

the eastern Mediterranean coast of what is now Syria and Lebanon. From their ports of Sidon and Tyre, merchants set out for the North African coast to buy gold, ivory, and slaves from sub-Saharan Africa. At first they established trading posts, but over time these became permanent and substantial settlements in their own right.

The Phoenician name for Carthage was *Kart-hadasht*, meaning "new capital" or "new city." It stands on a promontory on the shores of the Gulf of Tunis and is defended on three sides by the sea. On the fourth, landward, side, the Carthaginians built a huge defensive wall, 30 ft (9 m) thick and more than 50 ft (15m) high. Quarters for thousands of soldiers, their many horses and 300 elephants, were built nearby. The city had two excellent harbors: the oblong outer harbor, for merchant shipping, connected by a narrow channel to the circular inner harbor, which had berths for 220 warships. The basis of the city's wealth and power was trade: dates and animal skins from the Sahara; ivory, gold, and slaves from West Africa; grain and copper from Sardinia; silver from Spain; tin from as far away as Britain; and grains, wine, and glassware from Carthage itself. Such was the maritime trading strength of Carthage that some time before 400 BCE, the admiral Hanno took a fleet of 60 vessels out into the Atlantic Ocean and south down the west coast of Africa to the Gulf of Guinea and perhaps even to Gabon. Carthaginian navigators also sailed as far west as the Azores, as demonstrated by a cache of Carthaginian coins found on the islands.

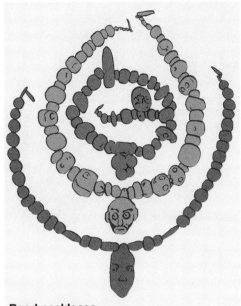

Bead necklaces
The Carthaginians had a passion for jewelry, and often wore cheap and gaudy trinkets which came from places visited by their trading ships, particularly the Mediterranean coast of North Africa.

Phoenician trade routes
The Phoenicians, who sailed from the ports of Sidon and Tyre on the eastern Mediterranean, set up trading posts with a view to forging a link with the slave, gold and ivory trades of sub-Saharan Africa. This map shows how many of these posts had developed into permanent settlements and cities by c.700 BCE.

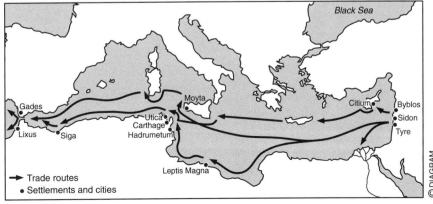

Black Sea

Gades
Moyta
Citium
Byblos
Sidon
Utica
Carthage
Tyre
Lixus
Siga
Hadrumetum

Leptis Magna

→ Trade routes
• Settlements and cities

© DIAGRAM

Domestic calm and foreign conflict in Carthage

Local currency
Most coins were roughly made and simply designed. Animals, palm trees and heads of Persephone were common motifs.

Contemporary style
Terracotta heads reflect the typical appearances of men and women in Carthage at the time. The woman is depicted wearing a long headdress, while the man wears a long beard but no mustache. Both men and women often sported nose rings as a form of facial adornment.

When it was first established, Carthage was a monarchy with a government similar to that of the Phoenician ports. A revolution abolished the monarchy c.450 BCE and set up a republic. The heads of state were two chief magistrates, known as *shofets*, who were both elected annually. Their main role was judicial, but they had the power to summon and preside over the two houses of parliament, where all political power resided. The senate, or upper house, acted as both legislature and executive, and its members were chosen exclusively from the aristocratic merchant families. The lower house was a popular assembly open to any male Carthaginian who wished to attend and express his opinions freely, but it had limited powers. While this system was open to abuse by the merchant families, who held power in the senate and appointed the senior judiciary, the Carthaginian constitution was so successful that it survived for almost 300 years without further revolution or dictatorship, and governed a population of up to 700,000 people, including many Berbers.

The inhabitants of Carthage lived in multi-storied houses that stood on very narrow streets. The ground floor contained shops and workshops, while the bedrooms were upstairs, with whole families often sleeping in one room. Sanitation was basic, and the city suffered from repeated epidemics. Wealthy Carthaginians lived on estates outside the city, surrounded by orchards, farms, and Berber villages. Carthaginian farmers grew almonds, figs, grapes, olives, pears, and pomegranates, while the Berbers provided such staple foods as cereals and vegetables. Cattle, sheep, goats, horses, poultry, and bees were kept. Mules and donkeys provided transport.

Carthaginian men wore long gowns with sleeves, and turbans or conical caps. They favored long, pointed beards and cut their hair short. Women wore long gowns with veils over their heads. Both men and women wore jewelry, including nose rings, and often used perfume. Many artifacts and statues were imported from Greece or made by resident Greek artists; in their own arts and crafts, Carthaginian craftworkers were much influenced by Greek designs, although their statues were more robust and heavier than the finer Greek works.

Conflict with the Greeks

The Phoenicians were not the only seafarers to settle in North Africa, for the Greeks also set up coastal colonies. In about 750 BCE, colonists from the Greek islands in the Aegean Sea established small settlements on the North African coast of Cyrenaica, in what is now eastern Libya, attracted by its fine climate and fertile, well-irrigated soil. They built the city of Cyrene in c.630 and, later, four more cities in the area, which they named Pentapolis (five cities). Like Carthage, all grew rich on trans-Saharan and Mediterranean trade. As they expanded their territory westwards, they came into contact with the Carthaginian empire, which had expanded eastwards along the coast. In c.321 the two agreed that Arae Philaenorum should mark their common border, but this truce lasted for only a few years. In 310 the Greeks invaded and conquered Carthage, but Greek rule over the city was short-lived, and they were expelled in 306.

The Carthaginians also came into conflict with the Berbers, who by c.250 had established three kingdoms in the region: Mauretania in what is now Morocco, Massaesylian Numidia in what is now Algeria, and Massylian Numidia along the border between Algeria and Tunisia, to the immediate west of Carthage. Carthaginians and Berbers had lived happily alongside each other for centuries, but in 203 the two Numidian Berber kingdoms united. Under King Masinissa (201–148 BCE), Numidia grew stronger and began to encroach upon Carthaginian territory. Although the Numidian kingdom broke up after his death, the Berbers continued to threaten Carthage, encouraged by an alliance with the third threat to that city, Rome.

The Greeks in North Africa
The Greek Empire expanded to include settlements on the North African coast, and reached its greatest extent c.550 BCE. Ensuing territorial disputes with the neighboring Carthaginians were settled c.321 when a boundary was established between the two powers. However, the Greeks invaded and conquered Carthage in 310, only to be expelled from the city in 306.

Carthaginian statuettes (right)
The dancing girl is crude in design and is an example of local workmanship. In contrast, the girl playing the double flute is much finer and was probably made by a Greek artist.

© DIAGRAM

The Punic Wars

Hannibal of Carthage
Hannibal was a skilled administrator and military leader who expanded Carthaginian power in Spain after its defeat by Rome in the first Punic War. However, his aggressive policy towards the Romans led to renewed war between the two powers in 218 BCE.

The Carthaginian empire
This map represents the greatest extent of the empire, c.264 BCE. In 149 the third and final Punic War broke out, and Carthage was destroyed in 146 by the Roman army under the control of General Scipio. The city then became a Roman province.

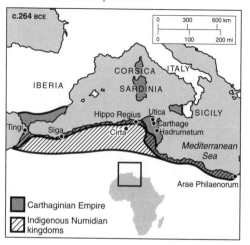

According to legend, the city of Rome was founded in 753 BCE, and by 272 had conquered the whole of Italy. It became a major Mediterranean sea power and thus a potential rival to Carthage. By this time, Carthage controlled an empire that included the whole of the northwest African coast, the Mediterranean coastline of Spain, and the islands of Corsica, Sardinia, parts of Sicily, and the Balearics. When, in 275, Carthage expanded its territory across Sicily to the Strait of Messina, facing mainland Italy, Rome went to war. The two cities clashed in 264 BCE in the first of what became known as the Punic Wars, so named from *Poenicus*, meaning 'dark skin' or Phoenician. By 241, at the end of a war fought largely at sea, Rome had expanded its navy sufficiently to defeat the Carthaginians, seize Sicily, and capture Corsica and Sardinia a few years later.

The two powers went to war again in 218 when the Carthaginian general, Hannibal, used his bases in Spain to invade Italy from the north across the Alps with a huge army, including many elephants. The Carthaginians were victorious in battle, notably at Cannae (216), but the Romans refused to surrender, engaging in a series of long campaigns that threatened Hannibal's extended lines of supply. After a series of defeats in Spain and Sicily, Hannibal withdrew in 203 to defend Carthage from Roman attack. He was finally defeated at the battle of Zama in 202 and the Carthaginians were forced to accept a humiliating peace settlement the following year. Spain became a Roman province, and Carthage lost control of all its territories apart from a small area surrounding the city itself.

In 149 the third and final Punic War broke out. Rome was by now at the peak of its Mediterranean power and sided with Numidia in its territorial dispute with Carthage. The Roman general Scipio, son of the victorious Roman general in the previous war, laid siege to the city and destroyed it utterly in 146. As a symbolic gesture, he sowed the site with salt. Carthage and its immediately surrounding territory then became a Roman province. A century later, the last Numidian king, Juba I,

Berbers and Phoenicians in North Africa

c.3000 BCE	Berbers established in North Africa
814	Legendary date for the foundation of Carthage by Phoenicians
753	Legendary date for the foundation of Rome
c.750	First Greek colonists settle in Cyrenaica
c.630	Greeks found city of Cyrene
c.600	Carthage becomes a fully independent state
509	Roman republic set up
c.450	Revolution in Carthage overthrows monarchy and sets up a republic
c.321	Greeks and Carthaginians settle their common border
310–306	Greeks conquer and rule Carthage
c.250	Three Berber kingdoms flourish
264–241	First Punic War gives Rome control of Sicily
218–201	Second Punic War leads to the second defeat of Carthage
203	Two Numidian Berber kingdoms unite as Numidia
201–148	Masinissa rules Numidia and begins to encroach on Carthaginian territory
149–146	Third Punic War leads to destruction of Carthage by Rome
148	After death of Masinissa, Numidian kingdom collapses, although Berbers continue to expand into Carthaginian territory
c.85–46	Juba I rebuilds Numidian kingdom
46	Romans depose Juba I and take control of eastern Numidia

The end of an era
King of Numidia 85–46 BCE, Juba I was deposed by Julius Caesar in 46 BCE and his Berber kingdom divided between Africa Nova and Mauretania.

was deposed by the Roman leader Julius Caesar in 46 BCE. Juba's Berber kingdom was divided into two parts. The eastern part was merged with Carthage to create the Roman province of Africa Nova, and the larger western part became part of the still independent Mauretania.

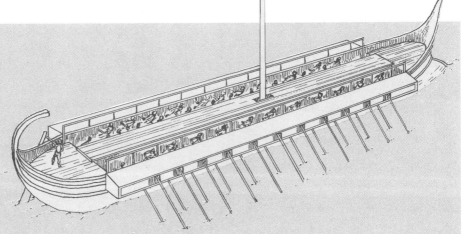

A Punic galley
Vessels like these enabled Carthage to become a sea power in the Mediterrranean, and were also a major asset in the first Punic War, which was fought largely at sea.

© DIAGRAM

Carthaginian gods and the afterlife

The Phoenicians who founded Carthage brought their religious beliefs with them, although they later added many foreign ideas and gods. Above all, they brought with them the idea of dual worship – the male and female in nature and the sun and moon in heaven. The Phoenician sun god Baal-Moloch they renamed Baal-Haman, while they renamed Astarte the moon goddess Tanit-Pene-Baal, or "Tanit who is the face of Baal."

Although the sun god takes precedence in most countries, in Carthage it is the moon goddess who is the most important. It is not clear why this was so, but Tanit was originally the moon goddess of local peoples before Carthage was founded, and so she was probably identified with the Phoenician Astarte when the first colonists arrived and given precedence in order to placate local people. The symbol of Tanit-Pene-Baal was a circle above a triangle with a bar between, probably representing a moon on an altar. She was represented in many ways, most commonly as a standing nude with her hands pressing her breasts as a sign of fertility, or a priestess standing in rich robes holding a dove and an incense box with two great vulture wings wrapped around her.

Baal-Haman, whose name meant "Lord of Heat" or "Lord of the Stone Pillars," was, like the moon-goddess, a compound of two gods: the original sun-god Baal and the local god Ammon, known in Egypt as Amun-Re. Few images of him survive, but those that do represent him as heavily bearded and wearing a robe with ram's horns projecting

Tanit-Astarte, the moon goddess
This sculpture formed the top of a sarcophagus containing a priestess' remains. The quality of the workmanship suggests that the artist was Greek, rather than Carthaginian.

Baal-Haman, the sun god
Second only in importance to Tanit-Astarte, he was usually portrayed as a bearded man seated on a regal throne.

from his head. Lower in rank than these two gods were deities such as Eshmun, the master and protector of the city itself, who bestowed wealth and health – his name translates as "to be fat" – and various baalim, or nature deities. They also worshipped Melkarth, originally a sun god but now regarded as the emblem of the national unity of the scattered Phoenician peoples. Every year a ship laden with costly offerings was sent to the temple in his home city of Tyre, in what is now Lebanon.

The Carthaginians built elaborate temples to their gods, as well as small, unadorned shrines, which were basically rectangular enclosures lined with upright stone slabs, like tombstones, dedicated to a particular god. These shrines contained no images of the gods, for the Carthaginians did not make graven images to worship. Like the Egyptians, they embalmed and buried their dead and made and buried grave goods for the afterlife, such as terracotta oil lamps, clay masks, and jewelry, although these items were far from grand, as if the living were too busy with their own lives to be sentimental about the next. The dead were also provided with basic food and drink for the afterlife.

The Carthaginians also offered human sacrifices to their gods, killing 200–300 first-born infants from the noblest families in order to win support from Baal-Haman in times of danger. Although such practices were not unknown in the Mediterranean region, the Carthaginians acquired a bloodthirsty reputation among their neighbors. Prisoners of war were also sacrificed in thanks to the gods for a victory. Such religious events were presided over by the many priests in the population, some of them holding hereditary positions handed down from father to son, or mother to daughter, as the female gods, including Tanit-Pene-Baal, could only be served by priestesses.

A tribute to the gods
This column is dedicated to both Tanit-Astarte and Baal-Hamaan, the two most important deities in Carthaginian religion.

Providing for the dead (below)
Carthaginians were embalmed after death and placed in sarcophagi (stone coffins not buried in the earth). Articles found in these tombs include: jewelry, a wine bottle, a mask to scare away evil spirits and a bird-shaped vessel to hold food or drink.

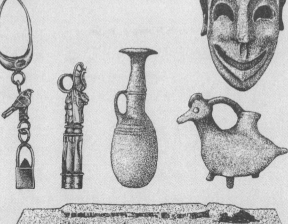

ROMAN NORTH AFRICA

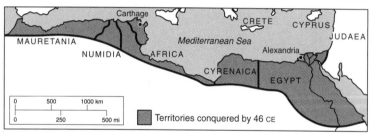

The Romans in Africa
The Romans expanded their empire to include North Africa. After the annexation of Carthage in 146 BCE the Romans moved eastward and conquered Egypt in 30 BCE. In 42 CE they annexed Mauretania. This map shows the territory occupied by the Romans by 46 CE.

A North-African-born Roman emperor
Septimus Severus (top) was born in Leptis Magna, a city in what is now northern Libya in 146 CE. He was a born soldier and became emperor of Rome in 193. He died in 211, and was succeeded by Marcus Aurelius Antoninus, (bottom) whose nickname was Caracalla.

According to legend, the Italian city of Rome was founded on its seven hills by the twins Romulus, after whom the city was named, and Remus in 753 BCE. Rome became a republic in 509 and gradually expanded its territory, overcoming the Etruscans and other local tribes to take full control of the Italian peninsula by 272 BCE. The three Punic Wars fought against Carthage between 264–146 led to the defeat of Carthage and Roman domination of the western Mediterranean, including the area immediately surrounding the now ruined city.

In 74 Cyrenaica became a Roman province and in 46, the last Numidian king, Juba I, was deposed by the Roman leader Julius Caesar and his Berber kingdom divided, with the eastern part merged with Carthage to create the Roman province of Africa Nova, and the larger western part becoming part of the still independent Berber kingdom of Mauretania. Ptolemaic Egypt fell under Roman control in 30 BCE, and Mauretania was finally overrun between 40–42 CE. In 44, Mauretania was divided into two provinces: Mauretania Tingitana in what is now northern Morocco, and Mauretania Caesariensis in what is now northern Algeria (Africa Nova was split into Numidia and Bycacena – the area around Carthage – in c.200 CE). By now the whole North African coastline was in Roman hands and the Mediterranean Sea had become a Roman possession.

Roman rule

In the four western provinces of the two Mauretanias, Numidia and Bycacena, the Romans established a number of cities, notably Leptis Magna in what is now northern Libya, and undertook massive engineering projects, such as the 31-mile (50-km) aqueduct to bring fresh water from a desert aqueduct to Carthage. The area exported olive oil, corn, and other produce to Rome, and was renowned for the many senators, officials, and lawyers it produced to serve the empire, as well as such scholars as St. Augustine of Hippo (354–430 CE). However, despite their overall dominance, Roman local control remained confined largely to the coastal areas, leaving the Berbers and others largely independent.

The two eastern provinces of Cyrenaica and Egypt followed a different pattern. The former maintained its close economic and cultural links with Greece and prospered from its Mediterranean and trans-Saharan trade links, while Egypt, once a proud and strong independent kingdom, was subject to administration by a prefect under the jurisdiction of the emperor and allowed no local autonomy. About 20,000 Roman soldiers were stationed in the province to subdue revolts, and local volunteers were pressed into service to run the administration. Industry and agriculture was improved, the cornfields of the Nile sending an annual shipment of grain to Rome in order to feed the imperial capital. Roman rule strengthened and enriched Egypt, but these measures were aimed at securing wealth for Rome, not at developing Egypt itself. Egyptian religion continued to flourish and indeed spread throughout the empire, while its culture and way of life remained largely immune to Roman influence.

Arch of Caracalla, 214 CE
This four-sided arch was situated at the meeting of four roads in the center of Tebessa, an ancient town in Algeria.

The largest amphitheater in Africa!
The Romans built an amphitheater large enough to accommodate 50,000 people at Thysdrus, near the Mediterranean coast. The town had grown in importance since becoming a center for the olive oil trade in the region.

End of empire

The Roman Empire reached its greatest extent during the reign of Trajan (98–117 CE), stretching from the Nubian border in the south to Scotland in the north, and from Morocco in the west to Mesopotamia in the east. This vast empire remained largely stable for the next 150 years, bringing peace and prosperity to North Africa and to the rest of the empire in Europe and western Asia. However, such a vast empire had long land borders to defend in central Europe, western Asia, and North Africa. During the third century these came under attack from hostile neighbors, such as the Sassanian Empire in Persia. Also, in the fourth century, Germanic tribes, such as the Visigoths and Vandals, were displaced from the lands along the eastern frontier in central Europe by the Huns, a nomadic and warlike people from central Asia migrating westwards in search of better food and pasture.

At first, North Africa was free from these incursions. The emperor Diocletian had abandoned much of northwest Africa to the Berbers in 285 and divided the

Trajan, emperor of Rome
An administrator b force of circumstance anc a conqueror by instinct, Trajan saw the Roman Empire reach its greatest extent during his glorious reign (98–117 CE).

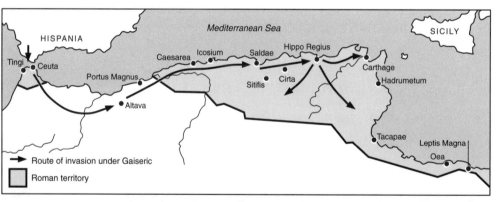

Mediterranean Sea
HISPANIA
SICILY
Tingi · Ceuta
Caesarea · Icosium · Saldae · Hippo Regius
Portus Magnus ·
Carthage
Sitifis · Cirta
Hadrumetum
Altava ·
Tacapae
Leptis Magna
Oea

→ Route of invasion under Gaiseric
Roman territory

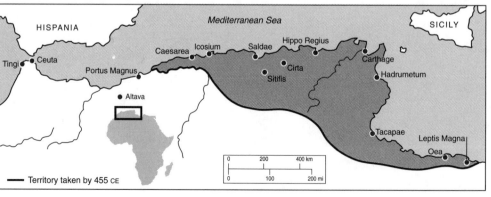

Mediterranean Sea
HISPANIA
SICILY
Tingi · Ceuta
Caesarea · Icosium · Saldae · Hippo Regius
Portus Magnus ·
Carthage
Sitifis · Cirta
Hadrumetum
Altava ·
Tacapae
Leptis Magna
Oea

0   200   400 km
0   100   200 mi

— Territory taken by 455 CE

The Vandal invasion
The Vandals, a Germanic people, swept down through the crumbling west Roman empire and into North Africa in search of new territory to conquer in 429 CE (top). Carthage itself was conquered in 439. By 455 most of North Africa had fallen under the control of the Vandals with the notable exception of the port of Ceuta (bottom).

entire empire in two in 286. Egypt and Cyrenaica were now governed from the eastern capital of Byzantium (later Constantinople, now Istanbul) and Carthage from the western capital of Rome. This situation lasted for more than a century, but in 406–09, as the western empire collapsed, the Vandals swept west and south through France and Spain, crossed into Morocco in 429 and captured Carthage in 439. The Berbers also took the opportunity to regain some of their traditional lands. In 476 the western empire finally collapsed, leaving the whole of North Africa from the Atlantic to the border of Cyrenaica in Berber or Vandal hands, with the sole exception of the port of Ceuta.

Byzantine rule

After the division of the Roman Empire and the fall of the western half, the eastern (or Byzantine) empire flourished. Good government and strong leadership kept the empire rich and intact, and well equipped to defend its borders and protect its citizens. During the reign of Justinian (527–565), the Byzantine empire went on the offensive to reunite the old Roman empire under its control. Taking advantage of conflicts between Vandals and Berbers, the Byzantine general Belisarius conquered the Vandal kingdom of North Africa in 533 and, by the time of Justinian's death in 565, virtually the whole of the North African coastline was in Byzantine hands. This period of stability lasted for almost a century.

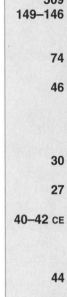

Roman and Byzantine North Africa	
753 BCE	Legendary date for the foundation of Rome
509	Roman republic set up
149–146	Third Punic War leads to destruction of Carthage by Rome
74	Romans take control of Cyrenaica
46	Romans depose Juba I, king of Numidia and merge eastern Numidia with Carthage to create Africa Nova province
30	Ptolemaic Egypt becomes a Roman province
27	Rome becomes an empire under Augustus
40–42 CE	Mauretania conquered by Rome, giving Rome control of the whole of the North African coastline
44	Mauretania divided into two provinces
117	Roman Empire reaches greatest extent
285	Much of northwest Africa abandoned to the Berbers
286	Empire provisionally split into east and west
395	Empire finally splits in two
429	Vandals invade Morocco from Spain
439	Vandals capture Carthage
476	Western Roman Empire collapses
533	Byzantine general Belisarius reconquers Carthage
565	Most of North Africa now in Byzantine hands

Justinian, emperor of Byzantium
During his reign (527–565 CE) he attempted to reunite the Roman empire.

The spread of Christianity

The Christian religion began in Palestine in about 30 CE, when its founder, Jesus Christ, was crucified for his beliefs by the Romans and his disciples began to preach his message throughout the Roman Empire. Traditionally, Christianity reached North Africa c.60, when St. Mark arrived in Egypt, but it is likely that there were already small groups of Christians in existence in Alexandria and elsewhere. Over the next 300 years, the new religion established itself in Cyrenaica, the towns and cities around Carthage, and in the far northwest.

Early Christian doctrine was not well defined, leading to differences of opinion within the expanding Christian world. Christians in Egypt, known as Copts, believed in the unity of both the human and the divine in the nature of Christ, a unity known as the Monophysite doctrine and rejected by other Christian churches. Further tension emerged within the Byzantine empire as the head of

A Coptic saint (above)
The first Christians in Egypt were called Copts. In 451 they established a church based in Alexandria which was independent of the Christian Church.

Christianity in Africa (below)
The tinted area on the map shows how far Christianity had spread in North Africa and the surrounding countries in 300 CE.

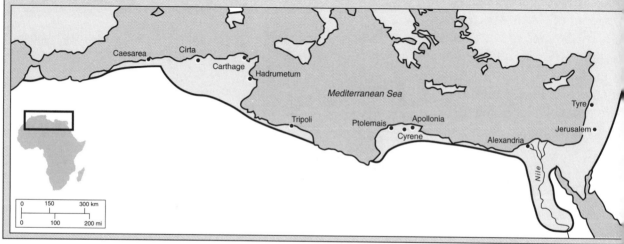

The Egyptian church in Alexandria, used to playing a leading role in the doctrinal councils of the Christian church, was increasingly expected to obey orders from the head of the church in Constantinople. Matters came to a head in 451 when the entire Christian church met at Chalcedon, near Constantinople, to standardize its doctrine and sort out its organization. Church leaders from Rome and Constantinople condemned the Monophysite doctrine of the Copts and declared that Christ had two separate natures. In response, the Copts took power into their own hands and established an independent church with its own Monophysite doctrines based in Alexandria, which they have maintained to this day.

Christianity in North Africa

c.30 CE	Death of Christ and foundation of Christianity
c.60	St Mark introduces Christianity to Egypt
100s	Coptic language emerges
200s	Romans persecute Copts
c.250–350	Life of St Anthony of Egypt, founder of Christian monasticism
304–305	Widespread persecution of Christians in Egypt
313	Edict of Milan tolerates Christianity throughout Roman Empire
324	Kingdom of Meroe defeated by Axum
391	Christianity becomes official religion of Roman Empire
451	Council of Chalcedon leads to founding of an independent Coptic church; Egypt and Axum adopt the Coptic rite
575	Nubia becomes Christian

A round tapestry
The god Horus is here shown on an ancient piece of threadbare tapestry astride his horse spearing Seth, his opponent. This image was adopted by the early Christians in Egypt as a means of portraying saints, such as St. George, vanquishing their rivals in battle.

Egypt and Sudan under Christian control

In the second century CE, the Copts developed a separate Coptic language based on a version of Ancient Egyptian with added Greek words written in a script derived from the Greek alphabet. Together, the Coptic language and religion ended the traditional Ancient Egyptian culture in a far more dramatic and effective way than the Romans were able to do. The old Egyptian religion was swept away, monuments were vandalized, and Egypt became one of three main centers of Christianity, alongside Rome and Constantinople. It was this new religion rather than any Roman identity that formed the glue that held Egypt together, as it did the other Christianized provinces in North Africa.

The Copts also had a huge impact on the development of Christianity. In about 270, a Coptic Christian, Anthony, gave away his large inheritance and became a hermit. He later went into seclusion,

Carved cross (above)
An example of a *crux ansata*, based on an Ancient Egyptian hieroglyph (or symbol) representing life, these crosses appeared from the fifth century onward.

Coptic church (right)
Built on an east–west axis, the nave (center) is separated from the side aisles by columns, and the south aisle is usually reserved for women. A screen, called a *haikal*, separates the sanctuary from the choir.

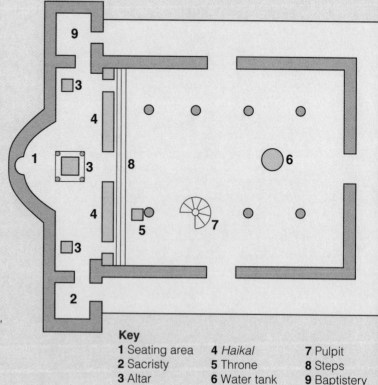

Key

1 Seating area	4 *Haikal*	7 Pulpit
2 Sacristy	5 Throne	8 Steps
3 Altar	6 Water tank	9 Baptistery

where traditionally he experienced every temptation to which humans are subject. A colony of hermits eventually gathered around him, which, after 20 years, he started to organize into a formal group, where the only communal activity was worship and meals. The rest of the time these early monks lived in solitude. St. Anthony's desert community later became the model for monastic orders throughout the Christian world.

Coptic icon
A statue created during the Coptic (or early Christian) period in Egypt, which lasted from about 200 to 642 CE.

The spread of Christianity across North Africa was not inevitable. The Romans persecuted Christians here as elsewhere in their empire, notably in Egypt under Emperor Diocletian in 304–305. This persecution failed to prevent the spread of the new religion; in 313, under the Edict of Milan, Christianity received official toleration in both halves of the empire and could be openly and legally practiced. In 391 Theodosius I forbade pagan worship and made Christianity the official religion throughout the Roman world.

Meroitic Sudan

The Meroitic kingdom of Nubia, which had remained independent from Roman rule, followed a different path. In 324 Meroe was defeated by its southerly neighbor, the Ethiopian kingdom of Axum, whose ruler, Ezana (reigned 320–355) had been converted to Christianity by missionaries from Christian Syria. Meroe then split into three small kingdoms: Nobatia, Makuria or Makurra, and

Alodia or Alwa, and its inhabitants gradually became Christian, influenced by the Coptic churches to the north in Egypt and the south in Axum. By 575, Nubia was entirely Christian, joining a Coptic world that stretched from Alexandria in the north down the length of the Nile valley to Ethiopia.

A relic from the siege (right)
This silver cross survived an attack by the Muslim army on Qasr Ibrim, a mountain in Nubia, and formerly a Christian diocese.

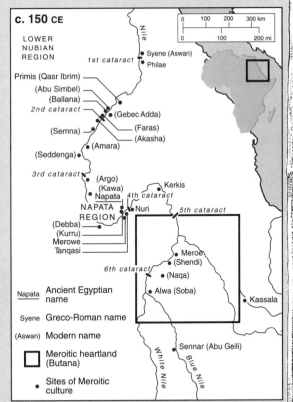

c. 150 CE

0   100   200   300 km
0   100   200 mi

LOWER NUBIAN REGION
Nile
1st cataract
Syene (Aswan)
Philae
Primis (Qasr Ibrim)
(Abu Simbel)
(Ballana)
2nd cataract
(Gebec Adda)
(Faras)
(Semna)
(Akasha)
(Amara)
(Seddenga)
3rd cataract
(Argo)
(Kawa)
Napata
Kerkis
4th cataract
NAPATA REGION
Nuri
5th cataract
(Debba)
(Kurru)
Merowe
Tanqasi
Meroe
(Shendi)
6th cataract
(Naqa)
Alwa (Soba)
Kassala

Napata — Ancient Egyptian name
Syene — Greco-Roman name
(Aswan) — Modern name
☐ Meroitic heartland (Butana)
• Sites of Meroitic culture

White Nile
Blue Nile
Sennar (Abu Geili)

The Meroitic kingdom
This kingdom grew out of the transfer of the residences and burial sites of the Nubian kings from Napata to Meroe c. 300 BCE. Its influence declined after 324 CE.

© DIAGRAM

THE ARAB CONQUEST

When Muhammad died in 632 CE, his authority extended over most of central and southern Arabia. Two years later the whole of the peninsula was under Muslim control, and Islamic armies were poised to break out into the entire Middle East. Palestine, Syria, Mesopotamia, and Persia soon became Muslim.

The Arab invasion

The conquest of North Africa began in 639, when Arab armies invaded Egypt. Alexandria was captured in 642, largely because of weak resistance and infighting due to persecution by the Byzantine authorities of the Copts, with their Monophysite doctrines. The Copts sided with the Arabs when they were offered freedom from persecution. Byzantine rule then came to an end and Egypt was ruled by Muslim governors appointed by the caliphs (rulers) in Medina, the political capital of the Islamic state.

After the capture of Egypt, the way was open to the rest of North Africa. Tripoli, in what is now Libya, was captured in 647, with the rest of Numidia and Mauretania following in 667, although fierce Berber resistance continued until 702, led first by Koseila and then by a woman warrior, El-Kahena (the feminine form of a word which means priest). Many Berbers then became Muslim

Muslim civilizations (right)
The Islamic empire was ruled by the Four Rightly-Guided Caliphs after the death of Muhammad in 632 CE. The empire in Africa extended westward under Umar and Uthman. The Ommayad dynasty took control and expanded the empire in Africa west along the Maghrib and into Spain. This map shows the situation in Africa in 711 CE.

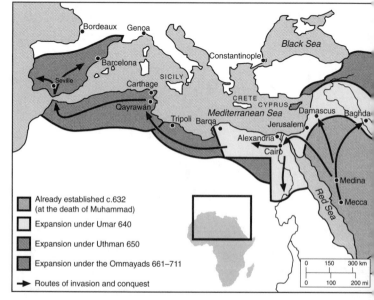

- Already established c.632 (at the death of Muhammad)
- Expansion under Umar 640
- Expansion under Uthman 650
- Expansion under the Ommayads 661–711
- → Routes of invasion and conquest

nd joined the Arab army. Carthage, the capital of Byzantine North Africa and the last city in Byzantine lands, was captured in 697, and by 711 Arab armies had reached the Atlantic Ocean and the Straits of Gibraltar. Here they prepared to invade Spain and western Europe, an invasion led by the Berber Tariq that took them into central France before their armies were defeated at the Battle of Poitiers in 732.

At first, many of the local religions, including Christianity, survived in this new Muslim and Arab empire. Islam does not particularly encourage, far less insist upon, conversion. The Qur'an urges Muslims to respect "the peoples of the book," that is, Jews and Christians. Gradually, however, Islam triumphed. Many people converted of their own free will, but forced conversion, sometimes of whole communities, taxes imposed on *dhimmis* (non-Muslims), and other measures under the Abbasid dynasty after 750 ensured that Islam eventually became the major religion of North Africa. Most importantly, adherence to Islam conferred social prestige and security, which led many to adopt it in order to survive and prosper under their new rulers.

Alongside the introduction of Islam came the increasing use of the Arabic language and script, which replaced Coptic as the official language of Egypt in 706. The Arabs were not opposed to local languages, however, translating the Qur'an into Berber in c.744. By 1000, merchants and *mahouts* (wandering preachers) had taken the new religion across the trade routes of the Sahara, turning the whole of North Africa into an Islamic region. Small communities of Copts in Egypt, Byzantine Orthodox Christians in the coastal towns, and Jews in the cities and in the Berber areas, survived, as did the Coptic Christians of Nubia and Axum, cut off from the rest of the Christian world by the Islamic empire.

Arabic calligraphy
"In the name of Allah, the Merciful, the Compassionate" is written below in four contrasting styles.

The art of the potter
North African potters often decorated their work with text from the Qur'an, the Islamic holy book. This example of the art is from Tunisia. At other times the images only resembled the actual script, as artists did not want the writings to be used for unholy purposes.

© DIAGRAM

Governing the new empire

Centers of learning
Centuries after the Arabs first invaded the countries of North Africa, the Islamic faith was further spread throughout the region by means of Sufi lodges, which housed students, guests and pilgrims.

At first the Arabs took over the existing political and administrative structures of the countries they invaded, although they did begin to build their own cities, notably Kairouan in modern-day Tunisia, their base for the conquest of northwest Africa and later its religious and political capital. New mosques were built, serving both as religious centers and administrative offices, but many former churches and temples were reconsecrated. The mosques also served as centers of learning, where students studied the Qur'an and *sharia* (Islamic law), grammar, Greek philosophy, mathematics, medicine, astronomy, and other subjects. Eventually, these studies developed into a syllabus comparable with that studied in medieval universities in Europe.

As the Arab armies pushed west across North Africa, it became increasingly difficult to govern this vast empire as a single unit from Medina. After Muhammad's death in 632, his rapidly expanding empire was ruled by the Four Rightly-Guided Caliphs (rulers) – Abu Bakr (632–634), Umar (634–644), Uthman (644–656) and Ali (656–661). After Ali's assassination in 661, the Ommayad dynasty, originally a family of merchants based in Mecca, took control, governing the entire Arab world from their new capital of Damascus in Syria.

The Islamic Ommayad caliphate was, by 715, the largest empire the world had ever seen, but it was unstable and undermined by theological divisions within Islam, which threatened its political and religious unity. In 750 the Abbasids from Persia overthrew the Ommayads, although they managed to retain control of Spain. The

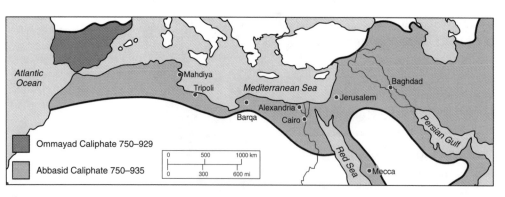

Atlantic Ocean

Mahdiya
Tripoli
Mediterranean Sea
Baghdad
Jerusalem
Alexandria
Barqa
Cairo
Persian Gulf
Red Sea
Mecca

■ Ommayad Caliphate 750–929

0	500	1000 km
0	300	600 mi

■ Abbasid Caliphate 750–935

The Abbasid dynasty
The Abbasids controlled North Africa from 750 CE, but lost their territories to independent Berber or Arab dynasties, such as the Idrisids, Alghlabids and Tulunids, by 935 CE.

Abbasids ran the entire Islamic world, including North Africa, from their new capital of Baghdad, but after 789, they too began to lose control, this time to independent dynasties, as it proved difficult to run such a vast empire from such a distant city.

Of these dynasties, the Idrisids ran Morocco from 789–926 until they were conquered by the Ommayads from Spain. The Alghlabids governed what is now Tunisia and Libya between 801–909, before they were replaced by the Fatimids – a dynasty of Syrian Arabs – while the Tulunids governed Egypt after 868. The Abbasids then managed to regain control of Egypt in 905 until they were expelled once again in 935, this time by the Ikshidids, who controlled the country until the Fatimids took control in 969.

Ibn Tulun
This mosque, or Islamic house of worship, was built in 876–879 and is the oldest surviving mosque in Egypt. Mosques follow a general pattern with a large open space protected by a roof, a *mihrab*, and a *minbar*. The *mihrab* is a semi-circular niche in one wall that indicates the direction of Mecca. The *minbar* is a flight of steps leading to a seat from which the preacher can address the congregation. Most mosques also feature a *minaret* which is a tall, slender tower with a platform at the top from which a *muezzin*, or crier, calls the faithful to prayer five times each day. Many mosques are elaborately decorated, with carvings and mosaic work.

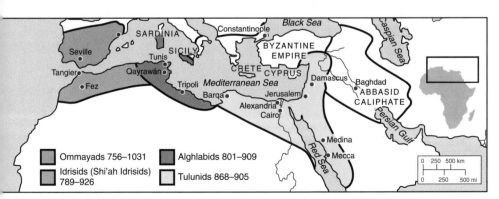

Muslim civilizations
This map shows the extent of the Arab empire c. 900. The Ommayads, Idrisids, Alghlabids and Tulunids all held considerable amounts of territory at some time between 756 and 1031 CE.

Ommayads 756–1031

Idrisids (Shi'ah Idrisids) 789–926

Alghlabids 801–909

Tulunids 868–905

© DIAGRAM

The Islamic faith

Islam is a monotheistic religion: believers accept only one god. The universe and everything within it are the creations of Allah, who is all-powerful, just, and merciful. The word Islam means "surrender to the peace of Allah," and Muslims give themselves up to Allah's will. They believe that Allah is the one true god and that Muhammad was his last prophet or messenger. Before him came other prophets recognized by Jews and Christians, such as Abraham, Moses, David, and Jesus. It was through Muhammad that Islam's teachings were revealed.

Muhammad was born in Mecca, in present-day Saudi Arabia, in 570 CE. Islamic teaching explains that while Muhammad was meditating one day, the angel Gabriel appeared and instructed him to serve as a prophet. He started preaching, and went on to become the leader of a religious community. In 622 Muhammad was forced out of Mecca by the hostile population and fled to Medina in what is known as the hijrah. He returned to capture Mecca in 630 but died two years later.

Islam's most sacred book, the Qur'an, is believed to be the actual words of Allah as revealed by Gabriel over a period of many years. The teachings and sayings of Muhammad and his followers were also collected and written down in the Sunna or Hadith, a vital source that helps Muslims understand the Qur'an better. Muslims laws, taken from both the Qur'an and the Sunna, are known as the sharia.

The five pillars

Islam rests on five duties that all Muslims must obey and carry out. These Five Pillars (supports) are based on the Qur'an and the actions of Muhammad, and dominate every aspect of a Muslim's life, as well as giving it a sense of purpose. The first pillar is shahadad, the Muslim statement of faith that "there is no god but Allah and Muhammad is His prophet." This belief is stated each day in the call to prayer. The second pillar is salah, the prayers that Muslims say five times a day. Wherever they are in the world, Muslims face towards the sacred Ka'aba in the holy city of Mecca to pray. The Ka'aba is a cube-like building into which is set the Black Stone, which Muslims believe

Islam today
The map shows the estimated number of Muslims in the world. Although the focus is on those areas in which Muslims comprise over 10%, and 50%, of the population, there are also parts of the world, such as North America for example, whose populations contain a significant number of Muslims but they are less than 10% of the total amount.

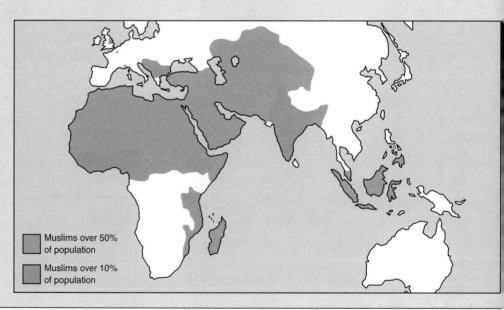

Muslims over 50% of population

Muslims over 10% of population

ll from heaven as a sign from god. The third pillar
zakat, the requirement of every Muslim to give
ne fortieth of his or her annual income to charity.
The fourth pillar is sawm, or fasting: during the
oly month of Ramadan, Muslims must not eat or
rink during daylight hours. The fifth pillar is the
ajj, or pilgrimage that every healthy Muslim must
ake at least once in their life to Mecca, during the
2th month of the Islamic year.

he mosque

lamic mosques, or houses of worship, follow a
eneral pattern in North Africa as elsewhere in the
lamic world, based on the first prayer-house built
Muhammad in Medina.

The divisions of Islam

About 50 years after Muhammad's death, Islam
split in two. The vast majority of Muslims —
including most in North Africa — are Sunnis, who
believe that after Muhammad's death, the caliphs or
rulers who succeeded him were his rightful successors.
Sunnis see the sharia, made by agreement of the
community, as their vital guide. In contrast, the
minority Shi'ahs believe that only the descendants of
Muhammad's daughter, Fatima, and her husband
Ali should succeed him and that after Ali died, God
sent imams or teachers descended from Ali as his
infallible messengers.

The hajj: the pilgrimage to Mecca
Healthy Muslims must make this pilgrimage, during the
twelfth month of the Islamic year, at least once in their
lifetime as a testament to their belief in Islam.

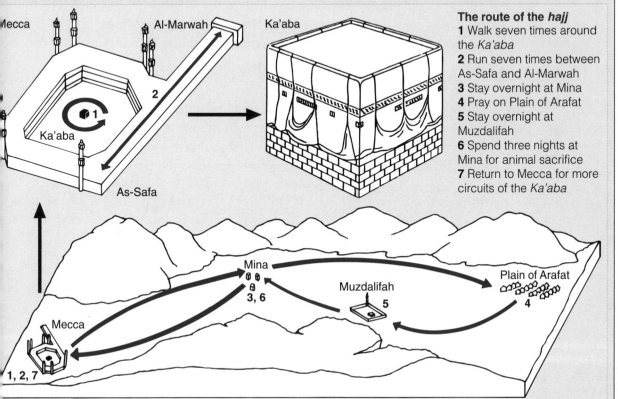

The route of the hajj
1 Walk seven times around the Ka'aba
2 Run seven times between As-Safa and Al-Marwah
3 Stay overnight at Mina
4 Pray on Plain of Arafat
5 Stay overnight at Muzdalifah
6 Spend three nights at Mina for animal sacrifice
7 Return to Mecca for more circuits of the Ka'aba

© DIAGRAM

THE MOORS

The Ommayads in North Africa (right)
Loss of interest in the Maghrib by the Fatimids enabled the Ommayads to expand into Morocco from Spain. This map shows the territory occupied by them 929–1031 CE.

Far away from the centre of Islamic power in Damascus and Baghdad, or from Fatimid control in Cairo, the countries of the Maghrib – what are now Western Sahara, Morocco, Algeria, and Tunisia – pursued their own paths and were more often linked with European Spain to the north rather than with neighboring African countries to the east. Unity, dismemberment, and foreign occupation are the three main themes that characterize the Maghrib in the 500 years after 900 CE.

In 926, the Ommayads took Morocco from the Idrisid dynasty. The Ommayads were originally merchants from Mecca and had ruled the whole of the Arab world from 661 until 750; they were then overthrown by the Persian Abbasids and expelled from all their lands except those in Spain. Here they established their kingdom at Cordoba, from where they set out to reconquer Morocco. Their control over their African territories was weak, however, and in 1031 a new dynasty, the Maghrawanids, seized control. Elsewhere in the Maghrib, the Fatimids of Egypt lost control of Algeria to the Hammadids in 1015 and Tunisia to the Zirids in 1041.

The Almoravids

This situation began to crumble in 1051 as the Fatimids of Egypt, allied with local nomadic Arab tribes, advanced into Zirid territory. In the western Sahara, a new nomadic Berber dynasty – the Almoravids – emerged in 1054 and

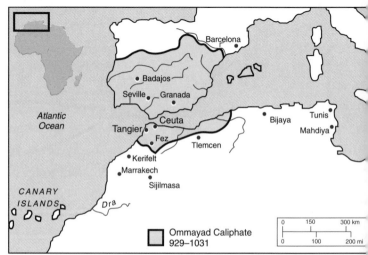

onquered the whole of Morocco by 1069, establishing
their capital in the new city of Marrakech in 1070. The
Almoravids started as a crusade launched by Yusuf Ibn
Tashfin, a Berber preacher who lived at the start of the
11th century. Tashfin preached that Muslims everywhere
had become too soft and were no longer following the
ways of Muhammad who, although not poor, had always
lived simply. Tashfin was an effective preacher and soon
collected a following of 30,000 warriors, known as
Almoravids. His army captured the major Moroccan
cities by 1069 and then split in two. One army headed
north to reinforce Ommayad Spain against its Christian
attackers, but eventually overthrew the Ommayad
dynasty itself, rather than supporting it. In the fighting,
many beautiful cities, including Cordoba, were destroyed
and thousands of books and other objects were burned. In
Spain, the Almoravids were known as Moors, not to be
confused with the present-day inhabitants of Mauritania.
The second Almoravid army headed south towards
Ghana, destroying the Ghanaian capital of Kumbi in 1076
and weakening the kingdom forever. By 1146, the
Almoravids had conquered a vast empire that stretched
from Barcelona and the slopes of the Pyrenean mountains
in Spain to the north down almost to the Senegal and
Niger rivers in West Africa in the south.

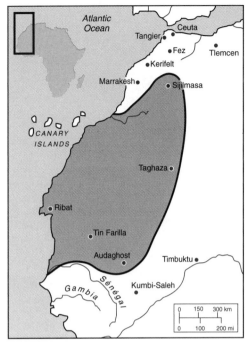

The Almoravid dynasty (above)
This map shows the extent of their territory in
northwest Africa in 1055 CE.

Muslims invade Spain (below)
A 12th-century illustration records one of
many naval invasions of Spain by Muslims
from North Africa between 700–1200 CE.

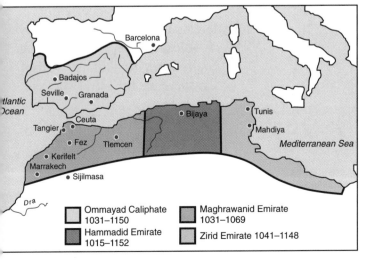

Ommayad Caliphate 1031–1150	Maghrawanid Emirate 1031–1069
Hammadid Emirate 1015–1152	Zirid Emirate 1041–1148

Other dynasties in North Africa (left)
Ommayad rule proved short-lived, as control
was lost to the Maghrawanids in 1031, the
Hammadids in 1015, and the Zirids in 1041.

© DIAGRAM

Almohads and Marinids

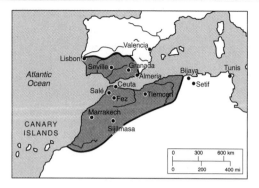

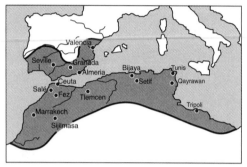

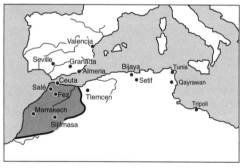

Expansion and decline of an empire (above)
The tinted areas show the extent of the Almohad empire at the following times: 1150 CE (top), 1172 CE (middle), and 1269 CE (bottom).

A mosque in Marrakech, 1147 (right)
The Almohad leader, Abd al-Mu'min, recaptured much of North Africa from the Christians, thus ensuring the revival of the Islamic faith.

The vast Almoravid empire was both unstable and weak, and in 1147 control of Morocco fell to another Berber dynasty, the Almohads. Like the Almoravids, the Almohads were basically a religious movement founded by Ibn Tumart in the Moroccan city of Tinmal. Once again, control of Spain changed hands, with the Almohads taking the country by 1172. Between 1152 and 1160, the dynasty expanded eastwards across the Maghrib, conquering Algeria, Tunisia, and Tripolitania (the western Libyan coast) by 1160.

Both the Almohads and their Almoravid predecessors minted their own gold coins, using gold brought across the Sahara from West Africa. As trade increased between Muslim North Africa and Europe, sub-Saharan gold found its way north: it has been estimated that as much as two-thirds of the gold circulating in Europe and North Africa in the 1300s came across the Sahara from West Africa, a trade helped by the spread of Islam throughout the north and west of Africa, and the unification of the Maghrib under its Almoravid and Almohad rulers.

The powerful Almohad dynasty, however, had many enemies, and in 1212 its army was decisively defeated at the battle of Las Navas de Tolosa by a Spanish Christian coalition led by Alfonso VIII of Castile, Sancho VII of Navarre,

and Pedro II of Aragon. By 1228, the Almohads were driven out of Spain altogether, and although a small Islamic state survived in southern Spain until 1492, Muslim power in the country was effectively ended.

After this crushing defeat, Almohad power began to weaken. Tripolitania and the eastern Maghrib were lost to the Ziyanid and Berber Hafsid dynasties by 1239, and Morocco was lost to the Marinids – originally a group of nomads – by 1269. Of these three competing dynasties, the Marinids emerged dominant, gradually taking over the whole of the northwest African coast as far east as Cyrenaica between 1336 and 1358 and attempting to reinvade Spain a number of times between 1275 and 1344, although the Ziyanids, Hafsids, and later the Wattasids, challenged them for control during the 15th century.

By this time Portugal and then Spain were establishing the first European colonies in Africa in ports situated along the Atlantic and Mediterranean coasts.

Crossing the desert (above)
Camels were introduced into North Africa by the Persians 2,500 years ago.

Almohad currency (left)
Silver *dirhams* which possibly originated in Fez, c.1163–1269 CE.

Gravestone (right)
This stone adorned the grave of Sultan Abu Yaqub, of the Marinid dynasty of Morocco, who reigned from 1286–1307 CE. Arabic inscriptions commemorate the dead king, and quote from the Qur'an.

North African rulers (below)
The map (left) illustrates the power-sharing between the Berber dynasties in North Africa in 1270 CE, and the map (right) the dominance of the Marinids in 1336 CE.

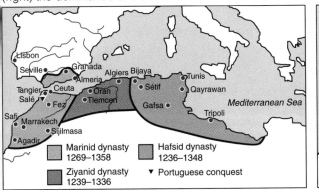

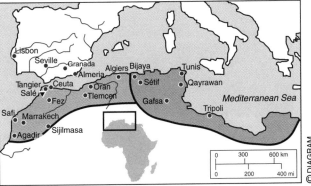

Marinid dynasty 1269–1358

Ziyanid dynasty 1239–1336

Hafsid dynasty 1236–1348

▼ Portuguese conquest

© DIAGRAM

The vanishing Jewish communities

Between the sixth and third centuries BCE, many Jews emigrated from Palestine to Egypt and what is now Libya. Their settlement was encouraged by the Egyptians to populate and defend border regions. Communities were eventually established across North Africa, with Jewish traders reaching Morocco by the second century BCE. Following a failed Jewish revolt against Roman rule in Egypt in 115–117 CE, the Egyptian Jewish community was destroyed. Survivors of this, and later waves of persecution, found refuge in the mountains of the northwest, converting some of the Berbers to Judaism. When the Arabs invaded in the seventh century, some of these Berber converts achieved notable military victories again.

Muslim rule

By 711 the Arabs had conquered all of North Africa, and Jewish immigrants from Palestine soon followed the Arabs into the region. In Egypt, the Jewish presence was re-established and by the 12th century numbered between 12,000 and 20,000. New arrivals from Palestine strengthened the communities and kept them in touch with religious developments. Under Muslim rule, the treatment of Jews varied. Some were pressured to convert to Islam, although most resisted the attempt, but it was not until the 13th century that Judaism was officially tolerated.

In 1492 Jews who refused to convert to Christianity were expelled from Spain and, in 1496, from Portugal. Many found refuge in North Africa. These Iberian Jews maintained a separate existence from the local Arabic-speaking Jewish communities and preserved their own Ladino language, a medieval form of Spanish using the Hebrew script. Following the Ottoman takeover of Egypt in 1517, and the extension of its empire across North Africa, discrimination against Jews was often harsh. Although the Ottomans continued to encourage Spanish Jews to settle in the region, Jews remained

The oldest synagogue in Tunis (above)
This synagogue was built over 600 years ago and is located in the Jewish quarter of the city. After the foundation of the State of Israel in 1948, and the corresponding rise in Arab nationalism, the majority of the Jews then resident in Tunisia left the country.

A safe haven (right)
Between 1492–1497 Christian intolerance of Judaism led to a period of Jewish emigration from Southern Europe and the Mediterranean to the towns and cities of North Africa.

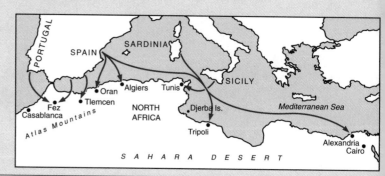

Jewish artisans (left)
This pestle and mortar, which originated from 19th-century Morocco, were made from brass and were used in the manufacture of cosmetics and medicines.

Out of Africa (right)
The figures show how many Jewish people in North Africa emigrated since the mid-20th century.

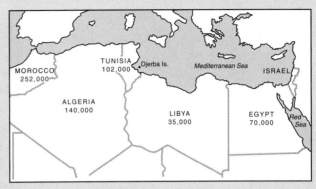

confined to ghettos and limited to practicing a few occupations. Nevertheless, the treatment of Jews was generally no worse, and sometimes much better, than that experienced by Jews in Europe at this time.

European rule

In the 19th century, much of North Africa came under European control. This brought great changes to the position of the Jewish communities and opportunities for them to improve their economic status. Occupational restrictions were abolished, enabling Jews to become teachers, doctors, lawyers, and even politicians, and Jewish merchants to expand into foreign trade and banking. Many identified closely with French culture, and Algeria's Jews were given automatic citizenship by the French, an act resented by Muslims denied this status. Others migrated to Egypt, where they were attracted by its tolerant environment and relatively wealthy economy.

The effect of Israel

The creation of Israel in 1948 and the rise of Arab nationalism had a devastating effect on Jewish communities. During the Arab-Israeli war of 1948, hundreds of Egyptian Jews were arrested and their businesses seized. Bombings in the Jewish areas of Cairo and Alexandria killed and injured hundreds. As a result, 25,000 of Egypt's 70,000 Jews emigrated by 1950. Most Jews, however, wanted to stay, but nationalist measures threatened their schools, businesses, and jobs, leading to the mass emigration of almost all Egypt's Jews by 1970. Elsewhere, Jews met with similar fates, most notably in Algeria, where almost the entire Jewish population of 140,000 emigrated within a few years of independence in 1962. Only in Morocco and Tunisia do Jewish communities remain, although much reduced in number. In Morocco, the total Jewish population fell from 270,000 in 1948 to 18,000 today, most of whom live in Casablanca, while in Tunisia it fell from 105,000 to just 3,000 in the same period.

Traditional clothing
This everyday costume is typical of that worn by Jewish girls in the 1930s in areas such as the Atlas Mountains of Morocco in North Africa. A long, striped garment (an *izar*), hung down to the feet and was worn over a colored blouse (a *derra*).

© DIAGRAM

67

MAMLUKS AND OTTOMANS

In 969 CE the Fatimid dynasty seized control of Egypt. The Fatimid empire had begun in the eastern Maghrib in 909 and had gradually expanded along the whole of the North African coastline, from Morocco to the Red Sea. The Fatimid rulers claimed descent from Muhammad's daughter, Fatima, as proof as their right to be caliphs (rulers) while their founder, Ubaidallah, claimed to be the Mahdi, or the divinely guided one, and preached an extreme form of the Shi'ah strand of Islam. Fatimid rule over Egypt was, initially, commercially and militarily successful: they built a new capital at al-Qahira (Cairo) and enjoyed good relations with their neighbors. After 1000, however, the Fatimids turned their attention more to the Middle East than to their North African possessions, and by 1100 had lost control over Algeria, Tunisia, and Libya. A succession of weak leaders further loosened their control over their large empire.

Ayyubid Egypt

In 1169, Atabeg, ruler of Mosul, a city in northern Mesopotamia, seized power from the Fatimids and made Saladin, a Kurdish warrior, governor of the province of Egypt. This new Zangid empire was, however, short-lived for Saladin had his own plans. Four years later, in 1173, he overthrew Atabeg and established the Ayyubid Sultanate, which soon stretched from Cyrenaica in the west to Mosul and the borders of Persia in the east, taking in the whole of Egypt, Palestine, and Syria, as well as the

The Hand of Fatima
Fatima was the daughter of Muhammad, and this "hand" is a symbolic representation of the five Pillars of Islam. These practices, based on the Qur'an, and Muhammad's actions, dominate every aspect of a Muslim's life as well as giving it a sense of purpose.

The Fatimids in North Africa
This map shows the extent of the Fatimid dynasty's control of North Africa in 969 CE. The dynasty held sway in the region until c.1000 when it lost control over some of its African territory as it began increasingly to focus on expansion in the Middle East.

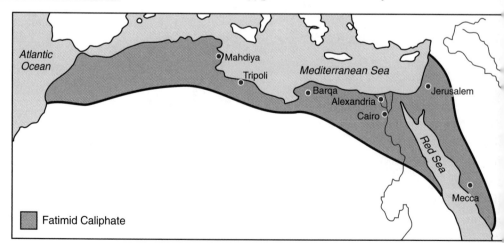

Atlantic Ocean

Mahdiya

Tripoli

Mediterranean Sea

Barqa

Alexandria

Jerusalem

Cairo

Red Sea

Mecca

☐ Fatimid Caliphate

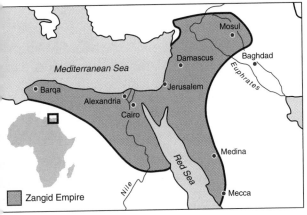

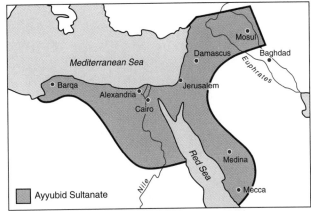

Zangid Empire and Ayyubid Sultanate
This empire was founded by the ruler of Mosul who took control of Egypt in 1169 CE. Saladin seized power in 1173 and founded the Ayyubid Sultanate.

holy cities of Medina and Mecca. Unlike the Shi'ah Fatimids, Saladin – whose name literally means "Welfare of the Faith" – was a Sunni Muslim and restored this form of Islam to Egypt. He was also a military commander of considerable ability, capturing Jerusalem and Acre from the Christian Crusaders who had occupied them. This provoked a third Crusade – a religious and military expedition – from Europe to defend Christian rule over these and other holy sites in Palestine. Although Richard I of England defeated Saladin in battle, he was forced to make a truce with him and failed to recover Jerusalem from Saladin's control.

Saladin, Sultan of Egypt and Syria
A powerful Islamic leader, Saladin (or, Salah ah-Din) united the wealth and learning of Egypt with the might of the Syrian army. He captured Jerusalem and Acre from the Crusaders who had occupied them, creating a powerful Islamic presence in the Holy Land which opposed existing Christian interests in the region.

Controlling powers in North Africa

969	Fatimids conquer Egypt and build new capital at Cairo
c.1000	Fatimid Empire at greatest extent
1015	Fatimids lose Algeria
1041	Fatimids lose Tunisia
1169	Zangid Empire seizes Egypt
1173	Saladin overthrows Zangids and creates the Ayyubid Sultanate
1193	Death of Saladin
1250	Mamluks overthrow Ayyubids and rule Egypt
1260	Mamluks defeat Mongols
1291	Mamluks evict final Crusader forces
1300s	Mamluk empire extends south into Nubia
1382	Mamluk empire declines
1517	Ottomans seize Egypt
1518–1519	Ottomans take Algiers from Spain and its hinterland from the Ziyanids
1521	Ottomans seize Barqa
1551	Ottomans seize Tripoli
1551	Ottomans seize Tunis and now hold the whole of North Africa except Morocco
1705–1714	Tunis, Algeria, and Tripoli become independent of Ottoman rule

© DIAGRAM

Mamluk Egypt

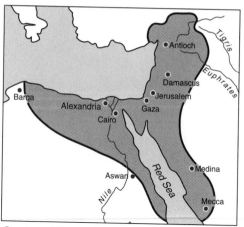

Center of the spice trade
During the 1400s the Mamluks gained control of the Red Sea trading routes, especially those to Mecca and Medina.

After Saladin's death in 1193, the Ayyubid Sultanate relied increasingly on its powerful army, manned largely by Turkish slaves known as Mamluks: the word Mamluk literally means "owned men." Islam preaches leniency in the treatment of slaves, and many Muslim commanders used large numbers of slaves – either bought or captured – in their armies. These slaves owed their lives to their military owners and were thus far more reliable than free soldiers, who often owed allegiance to tribal or regional leaders. However, many Ayyubid commanders were themselves Mamluks, which meant that the Ayyubid army increasingly became a law unto itself.

In 1250 the Mamluks seized power from the Ayyubids and ruled Egypt for the next 267 years. During this time, Egypt became the political, economic, and cultural centre of the Arabic-speaking world. The Mamluks defeated a large invading Mongol army at Ain Jalut in Palestine in 1260 and expelled the final Christian crusader forces from Acre, on the coast of what is now Lebanon, in 1291. For both these victories against infidel forces, they earned the support of all Muslims in their empire. They also revived the institution of the caliphate – the leadership of Islam – and installed a caliph in Cairo, as well as supporting the local rulers of Mecca and Medina, the two holiest cities of Islam.

At home, the Mamluks encouraged industry and crafts and restored Egypt's position as

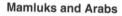

Mamluks and Arabs
The warrior on horseback is of Mamluk origin, whereas the soldier on the ground is Arabic. Although the Mamluks were originally slaves, they overthrew their Arab masters in the 1300s.

a center of the spice trade between the east and Europe. During the early 1300s, they extended their empire south into Christian Nubia and gained control of the Red Sea trading routes, especially those to Mecca and Medina. The effect of these victories was to expand Egyptian routes into Syria and along the Red Sea, and to defend Egypt's borders in western Asia and North Africa, thus ensuring the stability and economic strength of the state.

Two outstanding sultans – Baybars I (1260–1277) and Al-Malik an-Nasir (1293–1341) – were followed by a series of weaker leaders, causing the Mamluk empire to decline and its economy to falter, notably after the succession of Barkuk in 1382. Personal advancement in the state now depended more on ethnicity than on military skill, which led to series of defeats in Syria and elsewhere. The Ottoman Turks encroached from the north, while the Portuguese began to attack the former Mamluk monopoly of Red Sea trade.

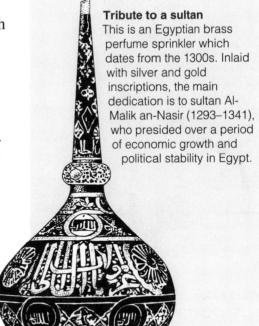

Tribute to a sultan
This is an Egyptian brass perfume sprinkler which dates from the 1300s. Inlaid with silver and gold inscriptions, the main dedication is to sultan Al-Malik an-Nasir (1293–1341), who presided over a period of economic growth and political stability in Egypt.

Tomb-mosque of Sultan Barkuk, Cairo
He succeeded to the position of Sultan of the Mamluk empire in 1382, but under his leadership its economy faltered and the empire declined.

© DIAGRAM

Ottoman expansion

Selim I Yavuz, or Selim the Grim!
An Ottoman sultan who lived from 1460–1520, he reigned from 1512–1520. Selim fought against the Kizilbash, Safavids and Mamluks and, perhaps most importantly, he gained control over the three main Islamic cities: Mecca, Medina and Jerusalem.

The military machine
This illustration shows a *janissary* (left) in traditional uniform and armed with a long spear, and a *sipahi* (right) armed with a lance, who was a member of the cavalry. *Sipahi* were feudal landowners who received grants from the state on condition that they provided military support whenever called upon in times of war.

In 1453 the Ottoman Turks had captured the Byzantine capital of Constantinople – ending the 1,000 year-old eastern Roman empire – and emerged as the most important power in the Mediterranean.

The first conflicts took place with Christian Spain, which in 1492 had conquered the Muslim kingdom of Granada in the south of the country and expelled all Muslims from the Iberian peninsula. The eastern Mediterranean then became a battleground between these two rivals. In 1511 Spain seized the city of Algiers from its Ziyanid rulers, leading the Ottomans to support the resistance to Spanish rule led by the Barbarossa brothers and other pirates. Meanwhile, Ottoman seafarers raided other Spanish-held ports in the region.

While this conflict went on, the Ottomans seized control of the eastern Mediterranean by conquering Egypt in 1517, thus ending Mamluk power. Spanish-controlled Algiers and its Ziyanid-controlled hinterland were finally overcome in 1518–1519, Barqa (Cyrenaica) fell in 1521, and Tripoli in 1551. With the capture of Tunis in 1574, the whole of coastal North Africa with the exception of Morocco fell under Ottoman control. In 1576 Ottoman troops attempted to conquer the desert region of Fezzán, south of Tripoli, but their hold on this remote and inhospitable region was never strong.

Although the Ottomans lost effective control over their Maghrib possessions between 1705 and 1714 and became rulers in name only, overall Ottoman dominance in North Africa remained largely intact until the very end of the 18th century, a period of almost 300 years.

Under Ottoman rule, Egypt lost its independence and became a province governed from the Ottoman capital of Istanbul (formerly Constantinople). The Mamluk sultanate was destroyed, but the Mamluks continued as a class. At first, Mamluks were appointed as viceroys, and although Ottoman troops were garrisoned in Egypt in case the viceroy rebelled, the Mamluk system of government and administration continued much as before, although tax revenues now went to Istanbul.

By the end of the 16th century, however, the Ottomans had tightened their control over Egypt, imposing their own governor and sending military and administrative personnel to run the country; from these groups, an executive council, the *diwan*, was formed to formulate and implement government policy in Egypt.

The Mamluks continued to import slaves who, as before, formed the core of the army, and Mamluks continued to be appointed to state offices. Gradually, the Mamluks infiltrated the Ottoman ruling class and eventually dominated it as they had the Ayyubid Empire some 400 years before.

Sulaiman's seal
This is the seal of Sulaiman the Magnificent, and is typical of the style of calligraphy which featured in his court.

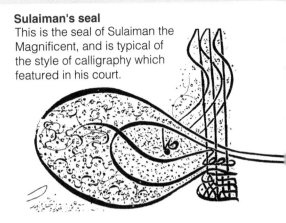

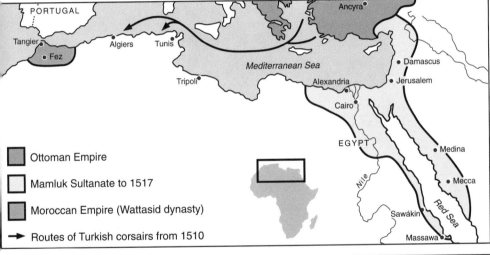

Ottoman Empire

Mamluk Sultanate to 1517

Moroccan Empire (Wattasid dynasty)

➤ Routes of Turkish corsairs from 1510

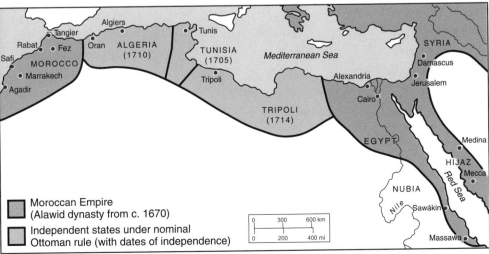

Moroccan Empire
(Alawid dynasty from c. 1670)

Independent states under nominal
Ottoman rule (with dates of independence)

The Ottoman Empire (1510–1715)
In 1510 corsairs carried out raids on Spanish possessions in the Maghrib (top left). By 1519 they had taken Algiers and its hinterland from the Ziyanids. Between 1517–1521 they had conquered northeast Africa as far as Barqa. By 1574 they had captured Tunis, and the whole of the north African coast (with the exception of Morocco), and part of Nubia, was under their control. Between 1705–1714 they lost much of their control over their Maghrib possessions (bottom left). They remained nominal rulers and their dominance of North Africa continued until 1798 when Napoleon invaded Egypt.

© DIAGRAM

Mamluk society

The Mamluk government consisted of two classes: ahl al-qalam *(people of the pen)* and ahl as-sayf *(people of the sword)*. The former consisted of scholars and scribes, who administered the Islamic law and staffed the vast bureaucracy of government and the tax system. The latter consisted almost entirely of Mamluks and filled all the highest offices of state – including the sultan and all the provincial governors – as well as the senior judiciary and the army. Thus Egypt was governed by an elite whose members were almost entirely of slave origin or descent. Absolute control over the army gave the Mamluks total control over the country.

The Mamluk army had three divisions: the Royal Mamluks were the personal property of the sultan; the Mamluks of the Amirs were the property of officers, most of whom were themselves drawn from the Royal Mamluks; and the halqah, or non-slave cavalry unit, that consisted of Mamluk sons and recruits from freeborn Muslims. All three divisions owed allegiance to the sultan, whose ability to maintain himself on the throne depended largely on the strength of the Royal Mamluks, who formed the core of the army and held all the chief offices of state.

The slave society

The Mamluk state gained its great stability and strength through a complex system of loyalties based on a common heritage and the common training required to become a senior Mamluk official. It aimed to produce a class of skilled warriors who, cut off from their homeland and family, would be completely dependent on the sultan or the officer who purchased them.

Slave merchants acted as agents for the Mamluks and bought large numbers of slaves – mainly adolescent boys – from central Asia and the Caucasus. Once in Egypt, the slave boys were quartered in special barracks and enrolled in a Mamluk school, where they learned horsemanship, military arts and, of course, the basic beliefs of Islam. Once they had graduated, they were given their freedom and assigned to whatever rank their purchaser could afford. This rigorous, if brutal, system, developed a strong esprit de corps, but also contained elements of rivalry and factionalism that could, if the sultan was weak, develop into anarchy.

Mamluk control extended throughout government, the army, and trade; they owned most of the land and dominated society. Non-Mamluks, such as religious scholars and scribes, were assimilated into society but the peasantry was excluded and posed a threat of rebellion if their needs were not met.

Mosque lamp (right)
This lamp bears the coat of arms of the emir Ala ad-Din the Bowman (1216–1285) who at one time held the position of governor of Egypt. The central motif is of two golden bows on a red background.

Preparing for conflict (above)
This illustration graphically portrays Mamluks exercising in the courtyard of a royal palace in Cairo. Brought as slaves primarily from Central Asia, the boys were housed in barracks, and enrolled in a Mamluk school where they learned military arts, horsemanship, and the principles of the Islamic faith.

An Egyptian man-of-war (right)
This illustration of a river boat, bearing three archers, dates from the period when the Mamluks controlled Egypt. Made from painted leather, the image featured in shadow plays which were popular in Egypt in the 15th century.

The Ottoman Empire

The Ottomans were a Turkish Muslim tribe who, under Osman I (reigned 1280–1324), established a small kingdom in northwest Anatolia (modern-day Turkey). In 1354 Ottoman troops crossed the Bosphorus into Europe and captured Gallipoli, later seizing Adrianople which, under its new name of Edirne, became the capital of their fast-growing empire. The Ottomans then took Greece and Bulgaria and, in 1389, defeated the Serbs at Kosovo. By 1396 they had conquered all the Balkans and reached the southern banks of the Danube. Expansion into central Europe was halted at Belgrade by the Hungarians in 1456.

By this time, the Ottomans had established full control over Anatolia and, in 1453, had captured

Sulaiman the Magnificent (1494–1566)

Under his control, Ottoman power reached its peak, extending as far as Austria in the north and Persia in the east, with his navy in control of both the Persian Gulf and the Mediterranean. The 10th Sultan, he reigned for 46 years, and died on active service in Hungary. Although remembered for his military prowess in the West, the Islamic world knows him better in the domestic role of lawgiver.

he Byzantine capital of
Constantinople, finally ending the
Eastern Roman Empire that had been
set up 1,000 years before. Under its
new name of Istanbul, the old
Byzantine capital became the center of a
vast Islamic empire. During the 16th
century, the Ottomans rapidly extended
their power: east across Mesopotamia to
the borders of Persia; south-east along the
Persian Gulf to the shores of the Indian
Ocean; south along the Red Sea and into
Egypt and Nubia; west across the
Mediterranean to the borders of Morocco;
and north into present-day Romania and
across the Black Sea to the Crimea. Victory
over the Hungarians at Mohács in 1526 gave
them control over most of central Europe,
although they failed to capture the Austrian
capital, Vienna, in 1529.

Ottoman power relied on the army, the senior
ranks of which were recruited from Christian

Surrender of the flag
Defeated by the Christians at the Battle
of Lepanto in 1571, the Turkish fleet
was forced to hand over its prized
Standard.

families in the Balkans. To fill the
ranks, Christian boys were forcibly
recruited into the army, converted to the
Muslim faith, educated in royal schools,
and then placed in the sipahis (cavalry)
or janissaries (infantry) of the army.
Much as the Ayyubids used Mamluk
slaves to maintain control, the Ottomans
tied many of the subject peoples of their
multiracial empire to them through a system
of rewards and punishments.

Despite its vast territorial size and military
prowess, the Ottoman Empire was inherently
weak. There was no legally accepted line of
succession for the sultan, which caused rivalry
and bloodshed each time a sultan died. At first,
the civil service appointed on merit, but by the
17th century both the civil service and the army
relied on hereditary appointments. The
government was often conservative and cautious,
although the empire was briefly reinvigorated by
the efforts of the Koprulu family of administrators,
who ran the government between 1656 and 1702.
During the early 18th century, the Ottoman Empire
entered a long but slow period of decline lasting more
than 200 years that saw it become "the Sick Man
of Europe" and lose gradual control of all its
possessions in Africa, the Middle East, and Europe.

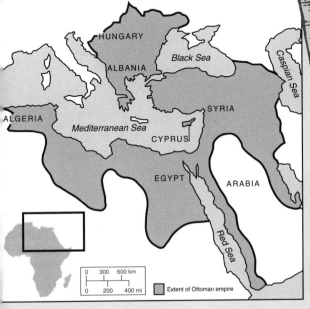

Extent of an empire
The Empire controlled three continents c.1566,
the year Sulaiman died, and its navy
dominated the Mediterranean, the Red Sea
and the Persian Gulf.

The Barbary pirates

The Brothers Barbarossa (above)
So named because of their red beards, Aruj and Kheir ed-Din were condemned by their victims as pirates but were in fact skilled seamen who became entwined in the conflict between Islam and Christianity in the early 1500s.

Nimcha (left)
This lethal sword, known as a *nimcha*, once belonged to an Algerian corsair on the Barbary coast in the 17th century. Its craftsmanship bears witness to the admirable metalworking skills of its Arab makers.

Under Muslim rule, the north coast of Africa was home to pirates who preyed on shipping from Venice, Genoa, and other Christian ports situated on the Mediterranean Sea. Christian Europeans called their Muslim opponents "barbarians", so these pirates became known as the Barbary pirates or corsairs – so-called because their activities were endorsed by the various rulers of the coast – and the coast became famous as the Barbary Coast.

The Barbary corsairs sailed in sleek galleys powered by sails and oars and capable of speeds of up to 9 knots (10 mph/16 kmph). Once a Christian ship was sighted, it was quickly overtaken, boarded, and overpowered. The corsairs stole whatever goods they could find, stripped the crew of their clothes and belongings, and sold them all into slavery in one of the North-African ports. Many members of the crew ended up as slave power rowing the Barbary galleys.

The two greatest Barbary pirates were Aruj and Kheir ed-Din, nicknamed by Europeans the Barbarossa brothers because of their red beards. The brothers led Muslim resistance to Spanish control over Algiers, seized by Spain in 1511. Kheir ed-Din placed the port under Ottoman control in 1518, although Aruj died in the fighting. Kheir ed-Din was made governor of the city and, as admiral of the Turkish fleet between 1533–1544, twice defeated the Genoese navy and raided the coasts of Spain, Italy, and Greece in search of loot.

By 1574 the whole of the Barbary coast was in Ottoman hands, although effective rule was in the hands of the corsairs. This allowed them a free hand to raid and pillage the northern (Christian-held) Mediterranean coastline and its shipping. Christians taken captive were often ransomed for vast sums of money, while the Barbary ports enriched themselves on the goods and slaves they captured at sea.

The main opposition to the corsairs was led by the corsairs of Malta, the strategic island in the middle of the Mediterranean, but during the 1680s a series of treaties between European powers and the Barbary corsairs began to limit their activities. During the Napoleonic Wars of 1796–1815, pirate activity rose again, leading to a determination to crush them once and for all. In 1804 a US naval force bombarded Tripoli, while in 1816 a combined British and Dutch fleet bombarded the main corsair stronghold of Algiers, forcing them to release all their prisoners and stop their activities. Fourteen years later, the French occupation of Algiers brought one of the most colorful and violent episodes of Mediterranean history to an end.

Warfare at sea
Although the Ottomans were not renowned as a great naval power they could muster a formidable force if the need arose. This illustration depicts the fleet asembled by Kheir ed-Din Barbarossa, who served the Sultan during the period 1534–1546.

© DIAGRAM

THE COLONIAL ERA

The port of Ceuta, on the Mediterranean coast of Morocco, was an important center for the trade in gold, ivory, and slaves. In 1415 the Portuguese occupied the town, giving it the dubious distinction of becoming the first European colony on the African mainland since the end of the Roman and Byzantine empires. Further east along the coast, Spain seized the port of Melilla in 1497. When Spain took over the Portuguese throne in 1580, Ceuta became a Spanish possession, a status both it and Melilla still enjoy today. Other Maghrib ports also came under temporary Spanish or Portuguese control at this time: Spain held Oran from 1509, Tripoli from 1510–1528, Algiers from 1511–1518, and Tunis from 1535–1574, as well as a number of other smaller Mediterranean ports, while the Portuguese took Tangier in 1471 and several other cities along the Atlantic coast.

A Portuguese carrack
This was a type of sailing ship which was often used by early explorers of the African coastline.

A Portuguese fort
Ships sailed regularly to India via the Cape of Good Hope, so the Portuguese built forts in order to safeguard the route. The fort illustrated is typical of one situated along the African coast.

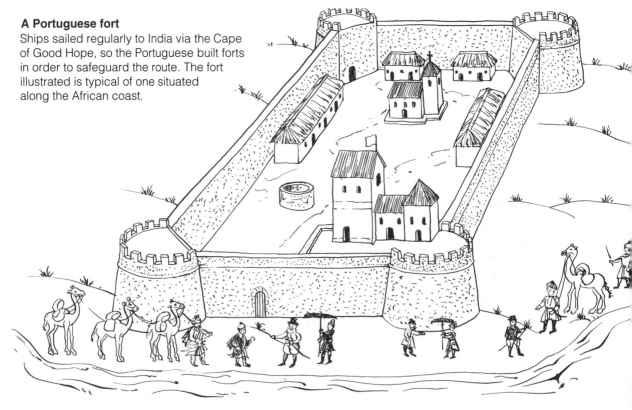

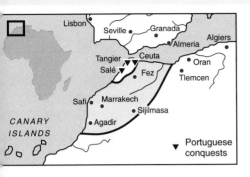

The Wattasids Sultanate
The tinted area on this map shows the area occupied by the Wattasid Sultanate in North Africa during the period 1472–1549.

European conquest of Africa	
1415	Portuguese take Ceuta
1497	Spanish take Melilla
1574	Ottomans control all of North Africa except Morocco
1578	Moroccans defeat Portuguese at the Battle of Alcazarquivir
1580	Ceuta passes to Spanish control
1705–1714	Tunisia, Algeria, and Tripoli gain virtual independence from Ottoman control
1798–1801	French occupy Egypt
1805	Under Mehmet Ali Egypt becomes independent
1821–1823	Egypt occupies Sudan
1830	French take Algiers and in 1831, Oran
1835	Ottomans re-establish direct rule over Libya
1841	Egypt accepts Ottoman sovereignty again
1848	Algeria becomes part of France
1860	Spain acquires Ifni from Morocco
1869	Britain, France, and Italy control Tunisian finances
1876	Egypt occupies Sudan
1881	French establish protectorate over Tunisia
1879, 1881	Egypt opposes Turkish rule
1882	Britain occupies Egypt
1882–1898	Independent Mahdist state of Sudan
1885	Spain establishes colony of Rio de Oro
1912	Morocco divided between France and Spain
1914	Egypt becomes a British protectorate

Independent Morocco

In 1574 the Ottoman Turks finally captured Tunis, giving them complete control over the whole of North Africa apart from Spanish-held Oran, which they captured in 1708, and Morocco, which from 1465 had been ruled by the Wattasid dynasty. In 1548 the Sa'dids supplanted the Wattasids and in 1578 defeated the Portuguese king Sebastian I at the battle of Alcazarquivir, ending Portuguese domination of the Moroccan coastline. Emboldened by this victory, Morocco began to create its own empire when, in 1591, it invaded the rich sub-Saharan kingdom of Songhay, from which it levied taxes. This vast empire was, however, unstable, and in 1610 Morocco split into two warring kingdoms, and remained divided until reunited by the Alawids in 1670.

Siege warfare
The crossbow could not be aimed with accuracy over long distances, but it proved invaluable in sieges and fighting at close quarters at sea. The weapon was used to great effect in defending Ceuta against Christians from the 12th century onward.

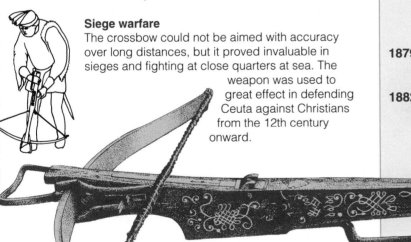

© DIAGRAM

European involvement

Napoleon in Egypt
During 1798–1799 the French, under the command of Napoleon, invaded Egypt to expand the French Empire, and to prevent the consolidation of the British Empire in India. Napoleon was later defeated by Admiral Nelson at the Battle of the Nile in Egypt.

Mehmet Ali
The *pasha*, or military leader of Egypt from 1805–48, he acted as an independent ruler and retained only nominal allegiance to the Ottoman sultan. He later occupied Sudan, and later Syria, and defeated the Ottomans in 1839. In 1841 he accepted the sovereignty of the sultan in return for his family becoming hereditary *pashas* of Egypt.

At the start of the 18th century, the Ottoman Empire began a long period of slow, but steady, decline. Local governors asserted their independence from Constantinople, with Tunisia (1705), Algeria (1710) and Tripoli (1714) becoming in effect independent countries with the Ottomans retaining only nominal rule. Only Egypt remained under direct Ottoman control. Apart from the two remaining Spanish ports in the Maghrib, the whole of North Africa was to remain free from European control for the whole of the 18th century.

This situation changed in 1798, when Napoleon Bonaparte, later to become Emperor of France, invaded Egypt in an attempt to create an overseas French empire and deny Britain an overland route to its own expanding empire in India. His plans were ended however, by Admiral Nelson and the British navy, which destroyed his fleet at the Battle of the Nile. The remaining French forces were thrown out by a combined British and Ottoman force in 1801.

Ottoman rule over Egypt was short-lived, however. In 1805 Mehmet Ali, an Albanian by birth who had commanded one of the Ottoman armies against the French, became *pasha* or viceroy of Egypt and effective ruler of the country, giving only nominal allegiance to the Ottoman sultan. In 1821–1823 he invaded and occupied Sudan, later occupying Syria in 1831–1833, and defeating the Ottoman army in battle in 1839. European powers worried about the decline in Ottoman power then forced him in 1841 to agree to accept the sovereignty of the Ottoman sultan in return for his family becoming recognized as hereditary *pashas* of Egypt. He died in 1849.

By this time, other parts of North Africa were falling under foreign control. In 1830 the French occupied Algiers and, in 1831, Oran, so gradually extending their control inland from the coast. The first French settlers arrived in 1834 and, in 1848, Algeria became an integral part of France. In 1835, the Ottoman Empire reasserted its control over Libya, imposing direct rule once again. Further along the coast, the heavy debts run up by the *bey* (governor) of Tunis led to Britain, France, and Italy aking over control of the country's finances in 1869. Tunisian attacks on French Algeria during the 1870s ed to the French invasion and occupation of the province in 1881.

Egypt and Sudan

In 1859 work began on building the Suez Canal, connecting the Mediterranean to the Red Sea. The canal opened in 1869 but, in 1875, the Egyptian government sold its shares to Britain, which was anxious to protect its vital communication routes to its empire in India. A nationalist revolt against Turkish rule then broke out in 1879, followed by a second revolt in 1881 led by Arabi Pasha, a colonel in the Egyptian army. At the request of the Egyptian government, a joint British-French force intervened in 1882 to put the rebellion down, inflicting a major defeat at Tel el-Kebir in 1882. British forces then occupied the Nile Delta, extending their control throughout Egypt by 1885 and into Sudan by 1898, which then became a joint Anglo-Egyptian condominium. In 1914, when the Ottoman Empire sided with Germany and declared war on Britain at the start of World War I, Britain made Egypt a British protectorate.

Raising the flag (above)
The tricolor is hoisted aloft by French soldiers at Tunis in May, 1881, to acknowledge the country becoming a French protectorate.

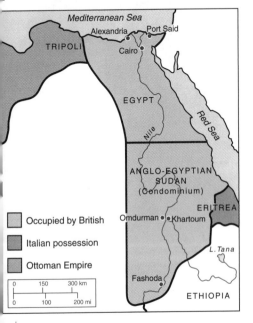

Legend:
- ☐ Occupied by British
- ■ Italian possession
- ▨ Ottoman Empire

0 150 300 km
0 100 200 mi

British expansion in Egypt and the Sudan (left)
This map shows the significant growth of British occupation, together with the land possessed by the Ottoman empire and Italy, in 1889.

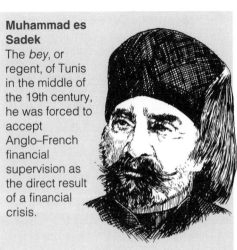

Muhammad es Sadek
The *bey*, or regent, of Tunis in the middle of the 19th century, he was forced to accept Anglo–French financial supervision as the direct result of a financial crisis.

© DIAGRAM

Strife in Morocco and Libya

As one of the few independent states in Africa at the start of the 20th century, Morocco attracted considerable attention from Spain, France, and Germany, each anxious to acquire a stake in controlling it.

Spain already held Ceuta, Melilla, and Ifni, originally seized by Diego García de Herrera, Lord of the Canary Islands, for Spain in 1476 but then abandoned in 1524 after several outbreaks of disease and repeated Berber attacks. Spain signed a treaty with Morocco to reacquire the port and its surrounding territory in 1860. Further south, Spain also acquired a protectorate over the coastal colony of Rio de Oro ("River of Gold") in 1885.

In 1906 an international conference in the Spanish city of Algeçiras – held at Germany's request – met to determine the future ownership of Morocco. The subsequent treaty recognized the authority of the Moroccan sultan, regulated French and Spanish intervention in the internal affairs of the country, but excluded Germany from any involvement in Morocco's future.

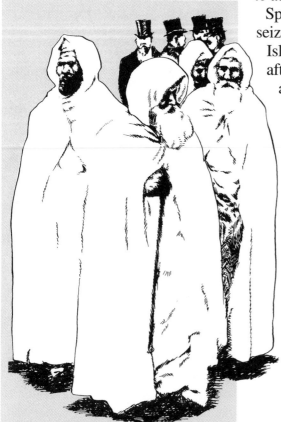

The Algeçiras Conference, Spain, 1906
The conference was set up at the instigation of Germany to decide whether or not the French or Germans should have control of Morocco. The subsequent treaty excluded Germany from any future involvement in the affairs of the North African country.

Ambush at Tidj Kardje (right)
Resistance to the French presence in Morocco was often fierce. This French army detachment was ambushed by Moors and resulted in the death of two officers and two non-commissioned officers.

Partition (left)

In 1912 Morocco was divided into French and Spanish zones. The Spanish zone was further divided into Spanish Morocco in the north and Spanish Sahara in the south. The map shows the situation in North Africa in 1933.

Augusto Aubry (left)

He was the naval commander when Italy invaded Libya in 1911, a rule not ended until 1942.

King Idris I (right)

He became the first leader of Libya upon achieving independence in 1951.

When Germany sent a gunboat to the Moroccan port of Agadir in 1911, the other two European powers decided to act. In 1912 the country was divided into French and Spanish zones, the Spanish zone divided into Spanish Morocco in the north and Saguia el Hamra, or Spanish Sahara, in the south.

The status of Tangier remained vague, but in 1923 it became an international zone administered by France, Spain, and Britain (Italy joined in 1928).

In 1911 war broke out between Italy and the Ottoman Empire, allowing Italy to seize Libya as part of its drive to acquire an African empire. By 1914, the whole of North Africa was under European control.

European Africa, 1914 (below)

Between 1899–1914 Ottoman power declined in North Africa, while colonial powers, such as France, Spain, Britain and Italy, expanded their territories.

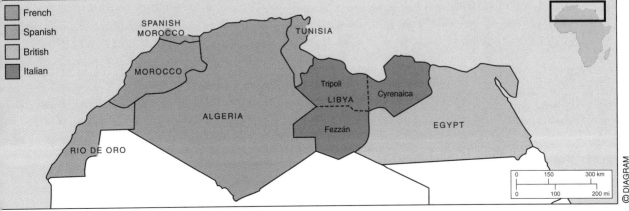

The Mahdist rebellion in Sudan

The Muslim Messiah
Muhammad Ahmad, also known as the Mahdi, led a revolt against Anglo-Egyptian rule in Sudan in 1882. After a series of battles, the state he founded lasted until 1898, 13 years after his death in Omdurman.

General Gordon
A former governor of Sudan (1877–1880), Gordon helped evacuate Egyptian troops in 1885. He died in 1885 at Khartoum while trying to hold the territory against Mahdist forces, despite the Mahdi's orders that his life be spared.

The struggle for control in the Sudan

1821–1823	Egyptian forces occupy the Funj kingdom and parts of Kordofan
1844	Birth of the Mahdi
1874	Egypt annexes Darfur
1876	Egypt occupies most of Sudan
1881	Muhammad Ahmad ibn Abd Allah proclaims himself Mahdi
1882	The Mahdi wins control of Kordofan
1883	The Mahdi controls Darfur and defeats British-led army at Shaykan
1884	General Gordon is besieged in Khartoum
1885	The Mahdi captures Khartoum; Gordon is killed
1885	The Mahdi dies, his successor continues his policy
1889	Mahdist army defeated on the Egyptian border by an Anglo–Egyptian army
1897	Belgian forces from the Congo defeat Mahdist army in the Upper Nile
1898	Kitchener defeats the Mahdist army at Atbarah and Omdurman; Sudan becomes a joint Anglo-Egyptian possession

In 1821–1823 the armies of Mehmet Ali, ruler of Egypt, invaded and occupied the Muslim Funj kingdom of eastern Sudan and Kordofan in central Sudan and gradually extended Egyptian control south towards Uganda and west into Darfur. By 1876 Egypt controlled most of present-day Sudan. Its corrupt rule was not popular, however, among many Sudanese, and in 1881 Muhammad Ahmad ibn Abd Allah, a Sudanese born in 1844 who claimed descent from the prophet Muhammad, proclaimed his divine mission to purify Islam and the governments that defiled it after he witnessed corruption in Kordofan. He called himself al-Mahdi, *the Mahdi,* or "right-guided one." With the support of the cattle nomads of Kordofan and Darfur, he won control of Kordofan and, in 1883, conquered Darfur and defeated a British-led Egyptian force of 10,000 troops at Shaykan, south of Khartoum.

By this time, the Egyptian government was seriously concerned about the situation. Two Egyptian attempts to capture the Mahdi had failed in 1881 and 1882, and so in 1884 the British government – effective controllers of Egypt since 1882 – dispatched General Charles Gordon to the Sudan to organize the evacuation of all Egyptian forces in the country. Gordon offered the Mahdi peace, but when that was refused, ignored his orders and tried to hold the territory against the Mahdist forces, which besieged him in Khartoum. When the city was captured in January 1885, Gordon was killed, despite instructions that his life be saved. An expedition from Egypt led by Lord Wolseley to rescue Gordon arrived two days after his death.

After the capture of Khartoum, the Mahdi established an Islamic state with its capital at Omdurman, across the Nile from Khartoum. Although he died the same year, his successor, the

Khalifah Abdullah, continued to expand the new state, threatening British and Egyptian interests in the Sudan and across North Africa. Successes against the Ethiopians in the east and in Darfur in the west were matched by failures in the north against an Anglo-Egyptian army in 1889, and in the south against an army sent from the Congo by its owner, Leopold II of Belgium, in 1897. A series of bad harvests and famines between 1889 and 1892 further weakened the country.

The greatest threat to the state, however, came from its location on the headwaters of the River Nile. British control of Egypt depended on control of these waters which, in the 1890s, were threatened by French expansion across North Africa from west to east. The British therefore decided to occupy Sudan. An Anglo-Egyptian force led by General Kitchener invaded the country in 1897 and, in 1898, defeated the Khalifah at the battles of Atbarah and Omdurman. The Mahdist rebellion was over, and Sudan became an Anglo-Egyptian condominium.

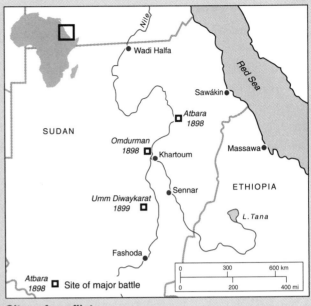

Sites of conflict
This map shows the major battles which took place in Sudan between the Anglo-Egyptian and Mahdist forces during the period 1898–1899.

Il est l'espoir de la France
Vive Marchand!

A diplomatic crisis
Captain Marchand and his French troops were forced to withdraw from Sudan in 1898 when confronted at Fashoda by an Anglo-Egyptian army under the control of Lord Kitchener.

Aftermath of defeat
The Khalifah Abdullah, who was the successor to the Mahdi, was defeated by an Anglo-Egyptian army led by Lord Kitchener at the Battle of Omdurman in 1898.

Desecration
The Mahdi's tomb was destroyed, his body burned, and the ashes thrown into the Nile by the British following victory at Omdurman.

© DIAGRAM

North Africa in World War II

In September 1939, Britain and France declared war on Germany after its invasion of Poland, leading to the outbreak of World War II. The French colonies of Morocco, Algeria, and Tunisia, as well as the British-dominated Egypt and Sudan, were therefore involved in the conflict. This situation was transformed in May–June 1940, with the German invasion and subsequent defeat of France, the establishment of the pro-Germany Vichy government in France, and the entry of Italy into the war on the German side. Vichy-held North Africa was now hostile to Britain, while the Italian colony of Libya posed a direct threat to Egypt. Above all, British communications through the Mediterranean

to Egypt, the Suez Canal, and on to India and its possessions in the Far East were under attack.

In pursuit of its ambition to construct a new Roman Empire in Africa, Italy invaded Sudan from newly-conquered Ethiopia in July and crossed the frontier from Libya into Egypt in September. The threat to Sudan was quickly lifted, but the battle for North Africa was to last for more than two and a half years. The Italian invasion of Egypt was soon halted and, by January 1941, British and Allied troops had taken the strategic Libyan port of Tobruk and were advancing along the coast towards the capitol, Tripoli. Alarmed at the full-scale Italian retreat, German troops under General Rommel

The North African campaign (1941–1943)
In September 1940 the Italians attacked British forces at Sidi Barrani. By February 1941 the British had expelled the Italians from Cyrenaica, and the Germans had entered the fighting (top). By June 1942 the Axis forces (Germans and Italians) took Tobruk. The First Battle of Alamein halted the advance of the Axis forces, and the Allies' success in the Second Battle hastened the fall of Tripoli in January 1943 (center). In 1942 US, British and Free French troops advanced eastward along the North African coast. By May 1943 the Axis forces surrendered.

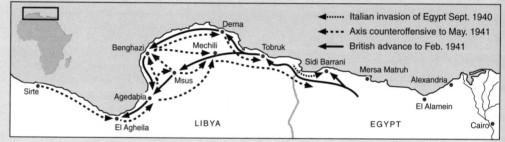

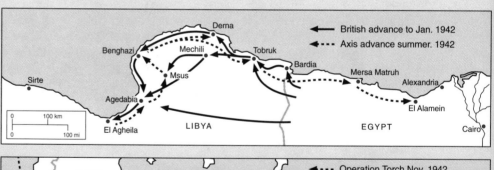

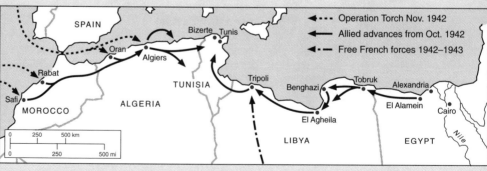

An unusual alliance

The Allies fought alongside the Egyptian Camel Corps against the German and Italian forces.

The conflict in North Africa (1939–1943)	
Sept 1939	World War II breaks out
June 1940	Italy joins war on German side
Sept 1940	Italians invade Egypt from Libya
Jan 1941	British push Italians out of Cyrenaica
Feb 1941	German troops land in Libya
June 1942	German forces capture Tobruk
Oct 1942	German Afrika Korps defeated by British Eighth Army at El Alamein
Nov 1942	Operation Torch – US and British troops land in Morocco and Algeria; Vichy French forces join the Allies as Germany occupies Vichy France; Tobruk recaptured by the Allies
Dec 1942	Allied troops enter Tunisia as Germans send reinforcements
May 1943	German and Italian forces surrender in Tunisia

landed in Tripoli and, with the help of their Italian allies, pushed the British back towards Egypt. For the next year, the battle for Libya swung back and forwards until British-held Tobruk was captured in June 1942. The way was now open to Egypt and the Suez Canal.

By October, British forces had been pushed back to El Alamein, only 50 miles from Alexandria and the Nile Delta. Here the British Eighth Army under General Montgomery fought a decisive 12-day battle that led to the first major British victory of the war. As the German army began to retreat westwards, Operation Torch landed British and US troops – the US had joined the war on the Allied side in December 1941 – in Vichy-held Morocco and Algeria on the other side of the continent and advanced rapidly eastwards. Free French troops fighting alongside the Allies advanced on Libya from the south. By April 1943, German and Italian troops had been driven out of Libya and were surrounded outside Tunis, where they surrendered in May 1943. The whole of North Africa was now in the hands of the Allies, and the war moved across the Mediterranean to Italy.

The battle for Libya

General Rommel and his German troops landed in Tripoli in 1941 after Tobruk had fallen to Allied troops, and the Italians had retreated along the coast. The British were pushed back toward Egypt, and Tobruk was later recaptured by the Axis powers in June 1942.

© DIAGRAM

THE STRUGGLE FOR INDEPENDENCE

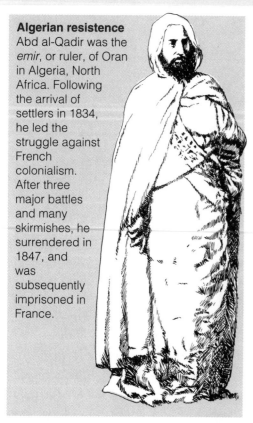

Algerian resistence
Abd al-Qadir was the *emir*, or ruler, of Oran in Algeria, North Africa. Following the arrival of settlers in 1834, he led the struggle against French colonialism. After three major battles and many skirmishes, he surrendered in 1847, and was subsequently imprisoned in France.

Despite the overwhelming technological and military might of the European colonialists, resistance to the imposition of colonial rule was strong, notably in the first half of the 20th century. In Algeria, Abd al-Qadir, the *emir* (ruler) of Oran, led strong resistance to French rule and the arrival of French settlers after 1834, fighting and losing three major battles and many skirmishes. After his surrender in 1847, resistance continued until 1852. Further revolts by the *Kabylie* resistance movement broke out in the east of the country in 1857. In Egypt, nationalist resistance was fierce between 1879 and 1882, first against Ottoman and then British rule, with further rebellions breaking out against the British in 1919–1920. In Sudan the Mahdi led a major Islamic revolt against Anglo-Egyptian rule after 1882, while in Libya, the *Sanusiyah* – a militant Islamic movement – resisted Italian rule from 1912 to 1932.

Morocco

The most effective resistance to European rule occurred in Morocco, the last North African country to become a European colony. As early as 1830, the Moroccans had clashed on their border with French troops from Algeria and fought a series of skirmishes until they were defeated at Isly in 1844. They also clashed with the Spanish at Tetuan in 1860 and again in 1894, when a tribal rebellion in the Rif mountains provoked a Spanish invasion. In 1909 attacks by Rif tribesmen on European settlers near Spanish-held Melilla on the coast prompted Spain to send a 50,000-strong army to end the conflict.

The establishment of French and Spanish protectorates over the whole of Morocco in 1912 prompted a series of revolts and uprisings across the country, notably in the Rif mountains in the north. In 1914 a local agitator, Bou Hamara, stirred up trouble against the Spanish. His rebellion was put down by a force led by a local tribesman, who in 1919 was poisoned on the orders of the Spanish military commander, General Silvestre. The tribesman's son, Muhammad ibn Abd al-Krim, then sought revenge. He captured 3,000 Spanish rifles and defeated a much larger Spanish army led by Silvestre at

A satirical view of Moroccan occupation
A German cartoon portrays the defeat of Spain at the hands of Abd al-Krim, observed from a safe distance by Britain and France.

the battle of Anual in June 1921. Silvestre committed suicide, 10,000 Spaniards were killed, and only 700 survived as prisoners. Further victories gave Abd al-Krim total control over the Rif mountains as well as most of Spanish Morocco.

In 1922 Abd al-Krim established a Rif Republic and was elected president. In early 1924 the Spanish tried, but failed, to recapture the area and were defeated at Sidi Massaoud in April 1924. As Abd al-Krim gained support, he pushed forward into French-held areas in order to link up with Berber tribes from the Atlas mountains in the center of the country. This prompted France and Spain to join forces and, in May 1926, a large army of 250,000 French, Spanish, and Moroccan troops led by Marshal Pétain, the French military hero of World War I, defeated Abd al-Krim in his stronghold of Targuist.

Abd al-Krim's campaign was not the only opposition to European control of Morocco. In 1912 Berber tribeseman rose in revolt against the French and defeated them in 1914 at El-Herri. Their guerrilla campaign continued until 1933, when they were finally defeated by the French at Jebel Sagho in the south of Morocco.

Abd al-Krim
A Berber leader, Abd al-Krim established a Rif Republic in northern Morocco in 1922, but was later defeated by a combined Spanish, French and Moroccan army in 1926 at Targuist.

Prisoners of war (below)
Attacks on European settlers near Melilla in 1909 prompted Spain to send a large army to suppress the rebellion, and imprison the defeated tribesmen.

Resistance to colonialism (left)
Many Africans took up arms against their colonial rulers soon after their territories had been occupied. In the first half of the 19th century the Algerians, under Abd al-Qadir's control, resisted the French between 1834–1847. In the west, Moroccan forces clashed with French and Spanish troops in an attempt to halt colonization; resistance lasted into the 1930s.

Map labels:

SPAIN · Mediterranean Sea · 0 200 400 km · 0 100 200 mi · Algiers · Bone · Tunis · Tangier · SPANISH MOROCCO · Tetuan 1860 · Oran · Sidi Ferrouch 1844 · Constantine 1837 · Melilla · Mascara 1841 · Anual 1921 · Isly 1844 · Biskra · TUNISIA · Atlantic Ocean · Rabat · Casablanca · Fez · Laghouat 1852 · El-Herri 1914 · MOROCCO · Marrakech · Figuig · Ouargla · Agadir · ALGERIA · Jebel Sagho 1933 · Ghadames · LIBYA · RIO DE ORO · Tindouf

Colonial borders 1933

Isly 1844 ◻ Site of major battle

▪▪▪▪ Boundary of area of resistance led by Abd al-Qadir 1834–1857

Bled el-Siba, an area that was only very loosely controlled by the Moroccan ruler

—·— Boundary of area of *Kabylie* revolts 1857

© DIAGRAM

A period of transition

Egyptian nationalists
Demands for the abolition of Egypt's former status as a British protectorate were achieved in 1923 when it became a constitutional monarchy.

Retribution
The scaffold awaits an African nationalist accused of assassinating an English official at Denshawi, in North Africa.

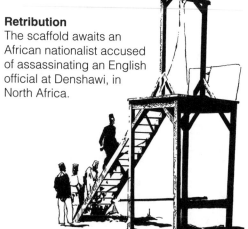

For all the countries of North Africa, the road to independence was far from easy. Egypt became nominally independent from Britain in February 1922. An Anglo-Egyptian treaty of 1936 provided for a British garrison for 20 years and the gradual withdrawal of British forces. Real independence for Egypt did not come until 1952, when King Farouk was overthrown by a group of army officers, one of whom, Colonel Nasser, later emerged as head of the new republic, established in 1953. Sudan gained self-government in 1953, and then full independence in 1956.

The Italian colony of Libya was occupied by the Allies in 1943, and placed under military government at the end of the war in 1945. In 1947 Italy renounced its claim to the territory, which in December 1951 became an independent kingdom under Emir Sayyid Idris al-Sanusi, who took the title Idris I.

Tunisia had a more difficult transition to independence. In 1920 the Destour party called for the creation of a national assembly. In 1934 Habib ibn Ali Bourguiba established the Neo-Destour Party and led calls for an end to French colonial rule. In 1938 all the leaders of the Neo-Destour Party were arrested and Bourguiba was imprisoned in France until 1942. Bourguiba was again

Nationalist conflicts in North Africa

1830–1844	Moroccans clash with French troops on Algerian border
1834–1847	Abd al-Qadir leads resistance to French in Algeria
1857	*Kabylie* revolt against French rule of Algeria
1860	Nationalist resistance to Spanish involvement in Morocco
1879, 1881	Nationalist revolts in Egypt against Turkish rule
1882–1898	Independent Mahdist state of Sudan
1909	Major rebellion in Rif Mountains against Spanish settlers
1912–1932	*Sanusiyah* resist Italian rule in Libya
1912–1933	Berber revolt against French ends in defeat
1919–1920	Nationalists revolt in Egypt against British rule
1921	Abd al-Krim defeat Spanish at Anual
1922	Abd al-Krim establishes Rif Republic
28 Feb 1922	Egypt gains independence from Britain
1923	Egypt becomes a constitutional monarchy
1926	Rif Republic overwhelmed by French-Spanish army
1934	Neo-Destour Party founded in Tunisia
1936	Anglo-Egyptian Treaty allows for British withdrawal
1938	Frances arrests leaders of Neo-Destour Party in Tunisia

Longevity
Spanish Sahara records General Franco's achievement as 25-year head of state.

arrested and detained in 1952, when further violence broke out. Self-government was granted in 1955, leading to full independence in March 1956. In Algeria, an eight-year war for independence broke out in 1954.

Morocco and Western Sahara

The situation in Morocco was complicated by the division of the country into French and Spanish protectorates and an international zone around Tangier. In 1953 France deposed the sultan, Muhammad V, because of his nationalist leanings, and replaced him with his more amenable uncle. French policy then changed, and in March 1956, French Morocco became independent, with the restored Muhammad V as sultan. Spanish Morocco – with the exception of Ceuta and Melilla – joined the new country in April 1956, as did the international city of Tangier. The Spanish-held enclave of Ifni joined in 1969.

Spain held on to its colonies of Rio de Oro and Saguia el Hamra (the southern section of its protectorate in Morocco), which it merged in 1958 to create Spanish Sahara, a province of Spain. The Spanish gave the colony independence in 1975, leading to an armed struggle for possession between Morocco and the Polisario independence fighters, which continues to this day.

Moroccan leader
Muhammad V served as sultan of Morocco from 1927–1957, and in the role of king from 1957 until his death in 1961. During the period 1953–1955 he was exiled by the French in Madagascar.

Peace
Women and children were caught up in the struggle for the liberation of the Saharan territories from Moroccan control in 2002.

1943	Libya occupied by Allies during World War II
1945	Libya governed by an Allied military government
1947	Italy renounces its claim to Libya
24 Dec 1951	Libya gains independence from Allied military control
1952	King Farouk overthrown in Egypt
1953	Egypt becomes a republic
1953	Anglo-Egyptian Sudan gets self-government
1954–1962	Algerian war for independence from France
1955	Tunisia achieves self-government from France
1 Jan 1956	Sudan gains independence from joint British-Egyptian rule
2 Mar 1956	Morocco gains independence from France
7 Apr 1956	Spanish Morocco and Tangier are restored to Morocco
20 Mar 1956	Tunisia gains independence from France
1958	Rio de Oro and Saguia el Hamra merge to create Spanish Sahara
3 July 1962	Algeria gains independence from France
1969	Ifni restored by Spain to Morocco
Dec 1975	After Spain withdrew from Spanish Sahara in Dec. 1975, the territory was partitioned between Morocco and Mauritania

Freedom fighters
This stamp, issued in 1963, records the ninth anniversary of revolution in Algeria.

© DIAGRAM

The fight for freedom in Algeria

A propaganda exercise
This poster was designed to promote peaceful coexistence between the French settlers in Algeria and the native people.

The French colony of Algeria attracted many settlers or colons, as they were known, from France and other parts of Europe, attracted by the available land and Algeria's close proximity to Europe. Algeria itself became part of metropolitan France in 1848, but it remained a two-tier society. The settlers were granted French citizenship automatically and had the right to vote, unlike the nine million Muslim Algerians, who found it hard to obtain citizenship and were denied any role in government. A few privileged Arabs had been naturalized in 1919 and given the vote, provided they abandoned their Muslim traditions. The remainder only obtained citizenship in 1944, and limited voting rights in 1947, when the French government promised Algerians a full share in the political and social life of their country, which would gradually pass under majority Muslim control. However, the vast majority of French people — and the French settlers in Algeria — agreed with their prime minister, Pierre Mendes-France, that "France without Algeria would be no France," and reforms were limited.

End of rebellion
Algeria became part of France in 1848, but the Muslim population were denied the right to citizenship and any role in government. Any opposition toward their French colonial masters was harshly punished. This illustration shows an execution in 1900 which took place at Sétif, Algeria.

Civil war
The failure of successive French governments to honor the promise of 1947 fuelled nationalist resentment against French rule. In 1943 the moderate nationalist Ferhat Abbas had called for an independent Algeria federated to France, but it was not until 1954 that leading nationalists formed the FLN (Front de Libération Nationale), which launched a guerrilla war on 1 November to win full independence from France.

At first the FLN was heavily outnumbered, its 800 fighters up against a French army of 20,000 soldiers. The FLN concentrated on isolated terrorist attacks, which met a violent French

Ferhat Abbas

A moderate nationalist, he was the first leader to call for an independent Algeria federated to France in 1943. However, it was not until November of 1954 that nationalists launched a guerrilla war to try to win full independence.

Guarding their territory

Armored troops guard against possible terrorist attack from the FLN, which managed to unite most Arab and Berber Algerians behind its campaign for independence in the mid-1950s.

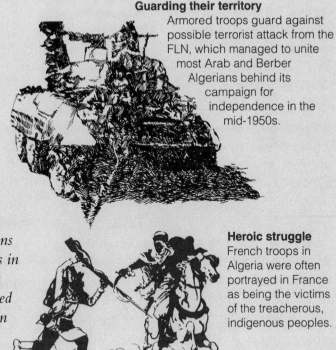

response, but which helped it to increase its own strength and unite most Arab and Berber Algerians behind its campaign. FLN attacks against settlers in Philippeville in north-east Algeria on 20 August 1955, in which 123 colons were killed, provoked the army to kill 12,000 Algerians in a retaliation the French governor-general, Soustelle, could not control. The conflict destroyed the land as well as killing people, as the French burned fields in try to starve the FLN and its supporters into submission.

Heroic struggle

French troops in Algeria were often portrayed in France as being the victims of the treacherous, indigenous peoples.

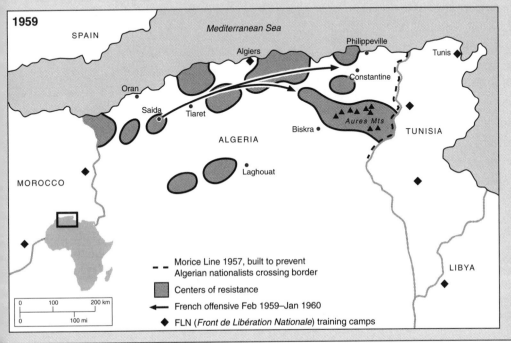

1959

SPAIN

Mediterranean Sea

Philippeville

Algiers

Tunis

Oran

Constantine

Saida

Tiaret

Biskra

Aures Mts

ALGERIA

TUNISIA

MOROCCO

Laghouat

LIBYA

- - - Morice Line 1957, built to prevent Algerian nationalists crossing border

Centers of resistance

0 100 200 km
0 100 mi

French offensive Feb 1959–Jan 1960

◆ FLN (*Front de Libération Nationale*) training camps

The Algerian resistance

Attacks on French military and civilain targets by the FLN (*Front de Libération Nationale*) in November 1954 were met with brutal reprisals. In 1959 an offensive by French forces ended when the French government acknowledged the right of Algeria to determine its own political future. However, renegade French soldiers and civilians continued to fight until 1962.

The Algerian civil war

At first, fighting was contained within eastern Algeria but, in the winter of 1956–1957, it spread to Algiers itself. In early 1957, the 10th Parachute Division under General Massu acquired police powers in the city, which were deployed savagely against alleged FLN members and supporters. The army's tactics alienated many ordinary Algerians, as it was obvious that the army was heavily biased in favour of the settlers and their campaign for L' Algérie Française (French Algeria) and was firmly against any proposals by the French government to negotiate with the FLN.

On May 15, 1958 a committee of settlers in Algiers threatened to seize power in Algeria from the French government with support from elements of the French army, which in turn plotted a coup in Paris against the elected government. The government exercised emergency powers to deal with this situation, but on 28 May the prime minister resigned and the Fourth Republic collapsed. General Charles de Gaulle, wartime leader of the Free French, returned to power as head of a new government. At first, it was assumed that de Gaulle would support the army and the continuing French ownership of Algeria, but when it was discovered in 1959 that he favored a settlement with the Algerians and was offering the FLN self-determination – which many feared would lead to independence – the settlers turned against him. Sections of the army attempted a military coup and mass riots broke out when de Gaulle visited Algiers in January 1960. The Organisation de l'Armée Secrète (OAS), a secret terrorist organization formed by the settlers and led by General Salan, former commander-in-chief of the army in Algeria in 1958 and then military governor of Paris, launched a second

General Charles de Gaulle
He was elected first president of the Fifth Republic in December 1958. French foreign policy under his control included granting independence to all French colonies in Africa, and negotiating agreements with Algeria, which achieved independence in 1962.

army coup on April 21, 1961, prompting the declaration of a state of emergency in both France and Algeria. As part of its murderous campaign, the OAS attempted to assassinate de Gaulle on 31 occasions and carried out numerous acts of terrorism.

The end of the war

Militarily, the French army remained in control of Algeria throughout the civil war, but it held only the major cities and could not control the vast rural areas, despite the success in 1959–1960 of the Challe offensive – named after General Maurice Challe, commander-in-chief of the army in Algeria and later leader of an OAS coup in April 1961 – against the northeast stronghold of the FLN. The conflict also tore French society apart, convincing de Gaulle of the necessity to end the conflict lest it cause a military coup, civil war, or revolution in France itself. In December 1961 he therefore began secret peace negotiations in Switzerland with representatives of the FLN, led by Ben Bella.

The Evian agreement, signed at Evian-les-Bains in France on 18 March 1962, agreed a ceasefire,

An insult too far
Riots against French nuclear tests in Algeria took place in 1960. Dummies, designed to measure the strength of the blast, were set up in the test zone.

installed a provisional Algerian government in Algiers, and promised a referendum offering Algerians the choice of integration in France, self-government in association with France, or full independence. When the referendum overwhelmingly supported independence, the French government handed over power to the FLN and Algeria became an independent nation on July 3, 1962.

The civil war had terrible results. Both sides had committed appalling atrocities, and many thousands of people had lost their lives. France was torn apart by the conflict, poisoning its politics for many years, but Algeria, while gaining its independence, lost most, as the nation was crippled at birth. The vast majority of colons, including nearly all the administrators, doctors, entrepreneurs, teachers, and

Ben Bella
After independence, he became prime minister of Algeria in 1962, and then president in 1963. However, he was overthrown in 1965 in a military coup, and kept under house arrest until his release in 1979.

technicians, fled the country, leaving the new nation short of men and women experienced in government and the professions. In addition, perhaps 150,000 Algerians who had collaborated with the settlers or fought in the French army – a total of 210,000 had enlisted – were killed in the troubled weeks after independence was granted.

The Algerian civil war

1923	Nationalist leader Emir Khaled deported
1943	Leading nationalist Ferhat Abbas calls for independence
1944	French citizenship granted to most Algerians
May 1945	Nationalist uprising in Sétif leads to mass bloodshed on both sides
1945	Nationalist leader Messali Hadj deported
1947	Algerians given limited voting rights and promised a share in government
1954	FLN (*Front de Libération Nationale)* formed
1 Nov 1954	FLN launches revolution for independence
20 Aug 1955	FLN attacks in east of the country kill 123 settlers; army retaliates by killing 12,000 Algerians
1957	10th Parachute Division gains police powers in Algiers
1957	Morice Line of electric fences and minefields built along border with Tunisia to block FLN supplies
13 May 1958	Mass protests against possible talks with FLN
15 May 1958	Settlers in Algiers threaten to seize power from French government.
28 May 1958	French prime minister resigns and Fourth Republic collapses
1 June 1958	General Charles de Gaulle takes power in France with emergency powers
October 1958	Fifth Republic formed in France
Feb 1959–Jan 1960	Challe offensive against FLN in north-east of the country
Jan 1960	Army revolt in Algiers and widespread rioting by settlers
21 April 1961	OAS army coup by General Challe in Algeria against de Gaulle
July 1961	Eight coup leaders sentenced to death
Dec 1961	Secret negotiations with FLN begin in Switzerland
18 Mar 1962	Evian agreements signed between FLN and French government
June 1962	OAS abandons struggle in Algeria
3 July 1962	Algeria independence after referendum favors independence; FLN takes power

© DIAGRAM

NORTH AFRICA TODAY

Independence at last
This stamp was issued in 1963 to commemorate the proclamation of the Algerian constitution.

At prayer (above)
Muslims in a North African town are shown praying to Allah. Islamic fundamentalism is growing in popularity in the early years of the 21st century.

Assassination (right)
While attending a military parade in Cairo on October 6, 1981, President Sadat of Egypt was murdered by Islamic fundamentalist gunmen.

Since North Africa became independent in the 1950s and 1960s – Egypt had been independent in theory since 1922, but its real independence dates from the overthrow of King Farouk in 1952 – the region has enjoyed considerable prosperity. The exploitation of natural resources, such as natural gas in Algeria and oil in Libya, and the development of manufacturing industries and tourism, have created countries with economies that are more diverse and stable than those of most nations south of the Sahara.

But modern North Africa faces many problems, not least the severe disparity of wealth between urban professionals and the largely rural or city-dwelling poor. The average income in the richest country, Libya, is only $6,700 (the average income is $29,080 in the US), while it falls to $2,090 in Tunisia, $1,380 in Egypt, and only $330 in Sudan. Wealth and wealth production remain concentrated in a few hands, with the vast majority of the population reliant on low-income work or casual labor.

Life expectancy rises from 66 in Egypt to 70 in Algeria, Libya, and Tunisia (76 in the US), but is only 55 in Sudan.

Fundamentalism

One of the main issues facing North Africa today is the rise of Islamic fundamentalism. The resources of the poorest country, Sudan, have been drained by a long civil war, caused by differences between the Muslim north and the non-Muslim south. Attempts to impose Islamic religious laws and penalties on non-Islamic people have been one of the main causes of the war.

Religious issues, too, have affected Egypt and Algeria, where many people support radical Islamic movements similar to those in Iran and other parts of the Middle East. They believe that Islamic fundamentalism is the best means of preserving their traditional culture. In Egypt, attacks on foreign visitors in the 1990s proved a major setback for the valuable and growing tourist industry. In Algeria, civil war broke out after the fundamentalist Islamic Salvation Front was banned after having won a general election in 1991. A year later, the military took over the government and suppressed the fundamentalists. By the end of the decade, more than 100,000 people had died in the conflict. Support for fundamentalism exists in other North African countries, although no major fundamentalist groups have so far developed in Libya, Tunisia, or Morocco, the richest countries in the region.

Political instability

With the exception of Sudan, the countries of North Africa are relatively homogenous in terms of population and religion. Yet most have failed to establish democratic institutions that satisfy the needs of their people. As a result, the region has suffered numerous, and sometimes violent, changes of government, many of them resulting from military coups.

Old and corrupt kings or hereditary rulers were thrown out in Egypt in 1952, Tunisia in 1957, and Libya in 1969. The first generation of nationalist leaders were also found wanting: in Egypt, when General Neguib was overthrown by Gamal Abd an-Nasser in 1954; in Algeria, when Ben Bella was overthrown in a military coup in 1965; and in Tunisia, when the aged and increasingly dictatorial Habib Bourguiba was toppled in a bloodless coup in 1987.

Religious fundamentalism and civil war have led to five military coups or uprisings in Sudan since 1958, as well as prompting the military to intervene in Algeria in 1992. In Tunisia, the government first legalized all opposition political parties in 1988 but banned the main Islamic party in 1992, and forbade all fundamentalist parties from participating in elections in 1994.

Only Morocco, under the successive kings Muhammad V (1956–1961), Hassan II (1961–1999), and Muhammad VI (1999–), has enjoyed continuity of government, although the constitutional monarchy established in 1977 is less than democratic.

Radical action
The Algerian government cancelled the second round of multiparty elections in 1991, fearing the popularity of radical Islamic fundamentalists. Rioting ensued and the fundamentalists ended up in a violent struggle with pro-government death squads.

Gamal Abd an-Nasser
He came to power in Egypt in 1954. His nationalization of the Suez Canal in 1956 led to French, British, and Israeli forces rapidly invading the country.

Habib Bourguiba
He took power and became the first prime minister of Tunisia from 1956–1957, and its first president from 1957–1958. He was later deposed by his prime minister.

© DIAGRAM

99

Arab conflict with Israel, and the future of Western Sahara

The Suez Crisis, 1956
Ships were deliberately sunk by the Egyptian navy to blockade the Suez Canal. Despite the efforts of the combined French, British and Israeli military forces, Egypt managed to retain control of the Canal.

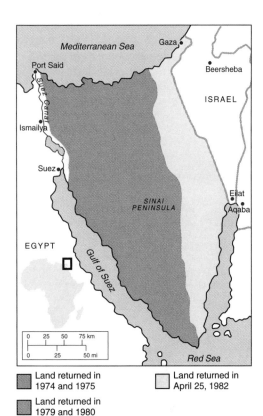

Land returned in 1974 and 1975

Land returned in April 25, 1982

Land returned in 1979 and 1980

Lost lands (above)
This map shows the areas of the Sinai Peninsula seized by Israel in 1967 and returned to Egypt from 1974–1982.

The establishment of the State of Israel in 1948 has dominated North African politics for the last half-century. Along with other Arab states, Egypt went to war to try to prevent the establishment of the new state in 1948.

War broke out a second time in 1956, after Britain and the US refused to fund the construction of the Aswan High Dam. President Nasser nationalized the Suez Canal to raise the necessary money, and then closed it to Israeli shipping. In retaliation, Israel invaded Egypt in collaboration with Britain and France, and then attacked the Suez Canal Zone in order to regain control of the Canal. International pressure forced all three to withdraw, making Nasser a hero of the Arab word.

Egypt, however, suffered a major setback in 1967, when Israel launched a pre-emptive strike against Arab nations threatening her borders, in what became known as the Six-Day War. The Israelis seized the Sinai Peninsula, and held on to it in 1973 after Egypt and Syria had attacked Israel in the hope of recovering Sinai and other lands lost in 1967. This second defeat caused the Egyptian government of Anwar Sadat to make peace with the old enemy. Sadat made a historic visit to Jerusalem, the Israeli capital, in 1977 and signed the Camp David accords in the United States with Israel in 1978, which led to a full Egyptian–Israeli peace treaty in March 1979. Egypt became the first Arab nation to recognize the state of Israel, although the treaty led to the assassination of Sadat by Muslim extremists opposed to his policies towards Israel. Since then, Arab North Africa has supported the Palestinian *intifada* (uprising) against Israeli occupation of their lands, and several countries, notably Libya, have supported Palestinian groups.

Support for terrorism

Both Libya, and to a lesser extent Sudan, have supported radical and extremist parties and terrorist groups around the world. The US accused Libya of supporting international terrorism and in 1986, after Libya had fired missiles at US military aircraft flying close to its shores, it bombed military bases in Tripoli and Benghazi.

Libya was also suspected of supporting those who had planted bombs on a Pan Am flight in 1988, which came down over Lockerbie in Scotland. The United Nations imposed sanctions on Libya in 1992 after it refused to hand over two suspects; they were eventually handed over to a Scottish court sitting in the Netherlands in 1999 and one was found guilty in 2001. Negotiations with Libya about compensation for the Lockerbie victims and the lifting of sanctions continued in 2002.

Despite Libyan condemnation of the terrorist attacks against the US in September 2001, and other conciliatory moves, Libya remains one of the seven countries in the world blacklisted by the US for supporting terrorism.

Western Sahara

The unresolved issue of Western (formerly Spanish) Sahara is a hangover from colonial days. This phosphate-rich territory was granted independence from Spain in December 1975, and Spanish forces withdrew in February 1976.

The Polisario – the Popular Front for the Liberation of Saharan Territories, backed by Algeria – then proclaimed the Sahrawi Arab Democratic Republic, but the country was quickly occupied by Morocco and Mauritania, which divided it between them. Recognition of the Polisario government by other African nations isolated Morocco, which left the Organization of African Unity (OAU) in protest at the action

The Polisario's daring guerrilla raids forced Mauritania to relinquish its claim in August 1979, allowing Morocco to occupy the whole country. Morocco built a defensive wall to keep the guerrillas out but warfare continued until September 1991, when the UN arranged a ceasefire. The UN tried to hold a referendum on the future of the country, but it was unable to draw up an electoral register acceptable to both sides.

Ten years after the ceasefire, the prospect of a referendum seems remote, and some UN officials are now proposing that Morocco's annexation be recognized in return for it granting autonomy to Western Sahara.

A lucky survivor
In response to suspected acts of terrorism by Libya, the US Air Force attacked targets near the harbor in Tripoli on April 15, 1986. Every effort was made to avoid civilian casualties during the air strikes.

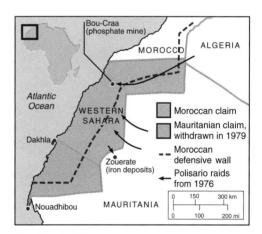

Conflict in Western Sahara
After the Spanish withdrawal in 1976, Morocco annexed the northern half of the country (with its phosphate mines), and Mauritania the southern half (with its iron deposits). Their forces were opposed by the Polisario who raided both countries.

© DIAGRAM

The Sudanese civil war

Ever since independence in 1956, Sudan has struggled with the seemingly intractable problem of reconciling the interests of the Muslim Arabs in the north with those of the black southerners, who practice either traditional African religions or Christianity. It has also failed to find a stable form of government, alternating shorts period of democratic rule with long periods of military dictatorship.

The civil war started in 1955, when an army unit from the south mutinied and began to fight the mainly northern-led government. In 1958 General Ibrahim Abboud led a military coup, abolishing all political parties. Abboud's view that the problems of the southerners could be solved by military, rather than political, action, angered many people. Especially criticized by people outside Sudan was the expulsion of Christian missionaries. In 1964 the problems of the south, combined with economic setbacks, intensified the civil war. A general strike succeeded in restoring civilian rule, but the new government was also unable to solve the country's

problems. In 1969 Colonel Gaafar Nimeiri seized power. He abolished all political parties and, in 1971, became Sudan's president.

In 1972 Nimeiri appeared to solve the problem of the south by giving the southern provinces autonomous regional government. However, in 1983, he changed his policies and abolished regional government, imposing Islamic law throughout the country. His actions sparked off a renewed civil war as the rebel Sudanese People's Liberation Army (SPLA) launched guerrilla attacks on government installations in the south. In 1985 army officers deposed Nimeiri in a coup. Multi-party elections were held in 1986, but the new government was weak. In 1989 Brigadier General al-Bashir seized power with fundamentalist support; he dissolved parliament and ruled through a military council, introducing the full Islamic penal code in 1991.

Sudan's new regime made attempts to restore peace in the south, but the fighting continued, which intensified to a considerable degree when the SPLA fought internally, with some arguing for independence while others wanted a

Colonel Gaafar Nimeiri (right)
Often regarded as the architect of an Islamic state, Nimeiri seized power in 1969. He abolished all political parties and, in 1971, became president.

Scene of conflict (left)
This map shows the main areas of activity during the civil war in Sudan during the period 1983–1993.

Map

SUDAN
- El Obeid
White Nile
Blue Nile
Nuba Mts
- Talodi
Bahr al Arab
- Malakal
BAHR EL GHAZAL
UPPER NILE
Nasir
- Wau
Kongo
ETHIOPIA
CENTRAL AFRICAN REPUBLIC
EQUATORIA
Yambio
Juba
- Torit
ZAIRE
KENYA
UGANDA

| 0 | 150 | 300 km |
| 0 | 100 | 200 mi |

Legend:
- Area of rebel activity
- Area of fiercest fighting
- SPLA "united" stronghold
- SPLA "mainstream" stronghold
- – – – Refugee centers
- **UPPER NILE** Southern regions of Sudan
- – – – Regional boundary

Victims of war
The civil war in Sudan prevented relief supplies from reaching the many refugees from Ethiopia, Chad and elsewhere, and resulted in great famine in many areas of the country.

united, secular Sudan. Many people suffered not only from the conflict but also through the starvation caused by the disruption of the production and distribution of food.

Following a ceasefire with some rebel groups in 1997, the government announced a referendum on the secession of the south, although no date was given and it was clear that the two sides would find it difficult to agree on a definition of "the south." The government also gave no indication that it might compromise on the imposition of Islamic law on the south. As a result the war continued, with the government launching a major offensive against the Nuba people of central Sudan. A six-month, renewable ceasefire was brokered by Switzerland and the US in 2002, leading to peace talks in Kenya.

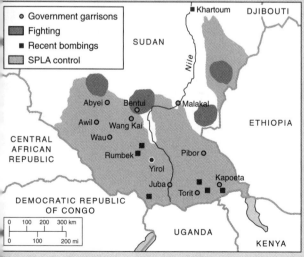

Disputes in the south
This map shows the disposition of conflicting forces in the southern part of Sudan at the start of October 2000.

The Sudanese civil war

1955	Army mutiny by Equatorial Corps in south of the country starts conflict
1956	Sudan gains its independence
1958	General Abboud overthrows civil government and heads military regime
1964	General strike leads to restoration of civilian rule
1969	Colonel Nimeiri seizes power and becomes president in 1971
1972	Nimeiri signs Addis Ababa Accords in Ethiopia, guaranteeing autonomous regional government to the south and ending the conflict
1973	Nimeiri's Sudanese Socialist Union (SSU) becomes only legal party
1982	Sudanese People's Liberation Army (SPLA) formed
1983	Nimeiri imposes Islamic law, sparking off renewed rebellion and conflict in the south
1985	Nimeiri deposed in a coup and a transitional government formed with civilian involvement
1986	Multiparty elections held: Sadiq al-Mahdi – great-grandson of the Mahdi – becomes prime minister
1989	Military under Brig. Gen. al-Bashir seizes power again with support from fundamentalist National Islamic Front (NIF)
1991	Full Islamic law reintroduced
1991	Southern rebels split along tribal lines and over whether to seek independence or a united, secular Sudan
1996	al-Bashir re-elected president and the NIF wins control of parliament
1997	Some of the smaller rebel groups sign a ceasefire with the government
1998	Government promises a referendum on the secession of the south
2001	Major government offensive launched against Nuba of central Sudan
2002	Six-month renewable ceasefire leads to successful peace talks in Kenya

© DIAGRAM

Coups d'État in North Africa

Independence from colonial rule by various European powers proved difficult to achieve for many African nations. Yet, once the battle for independence had been won, a variety of problems beset the new states.

As the maps show (right), some nations were subject to political instability and frequent military *coups d'état* after independence.

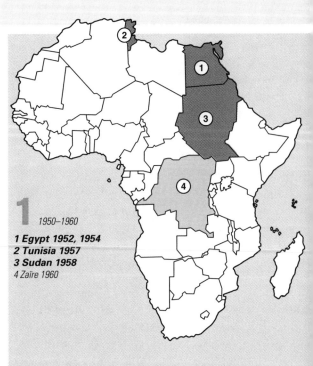

1 1950–1960
1 Egypt 1952, 1954
2 Tunisia 1957
3 Sudan 1958
4 Zaïre 1960

Abd al-Krim
Not all claims for independence were successful. The Berber leader, Abd al-Krim established a Rif Republic within Morocco in 1922 but, sadly, independence only lasted until 1926.

Coups d'état in North Africa

The only countries in this region of Africa not to have experienced a *coup d'état* in the last 52 years are Western Sahara and Morocco. Sudan has suffered five *coups d'état*, Egypt two, Tunisia two, Algeria two, and Libya only one. Leaders of some successful *coups d'état*, some of whom were later overthrown themselves, are shown below.

Muammar al-Quaddafi
He became leader of Libya, and also the commander-in-chief of the armed forces, in 1969 after a group of army officers overthrew King Idris I.

Houari Boumédienne
A former guerrilla fighter, he became president of Algeria in 1965 following a peaceful *coup d'état* which overthrew Ahmad Ben Bella.

Ibrahim Abboud
Seizing power in the Sudan in 1958, he abolished political parties and set up a military regime. In 1964 a general strike occurred and civilian rule was restored.

Colonel Gaafar Muhammad Nimeiri
He seized power in the Sudan in 1968, became president in 1972 and, in 1989, was deposed by disillusioned army officers.

Habib Bourguiba
Tunisia became independent in 1956 and, in 1957, he became president. Bourguiba himself was deposed in a bloodless *coup d'état* in 1987.

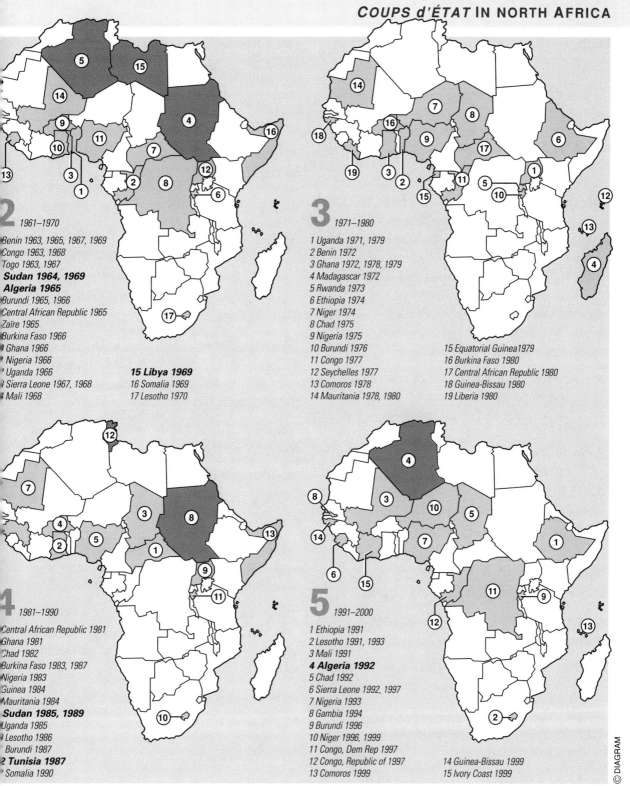

2 1961–1970

Benin 1963, 1965, 1967, 1969
Congo 1963, 1968
Togo 1963, 1967
Sudan 1964, 1969
Algeria 1965
Burundi 1965, 1966
Central African Republic 1965
Zaïre 1965
Burkina Faso 1966
Ghana 1966
Nigeria 1966
Uganda 1966
Sierra Leone 1967, 1968
Mali 1968

15 Libya 1969
16 Somalia 1969
17 Lesotho 1970

3 1971–1980

1 Uganda 1971, 1979
2 Benin 1972
3 Ghana 1972, 1978, 1979
4 Madagascar 1972
5 Rwanda 1973
6 Ethiopia 1974
7 Niger 1974
8 Chad 1975
9 Nigeria 1975
10 Burundi 1976
11 Congo 1977
12 Seychelles 1977
13 Comoros 1978
14 Mauritania 1978, 1980

15 Equatorial Guinea 1979
16 Burkina Faso 1980
17 Central African Republic 1980
18 Guinea-Bissau 1980
19 Liberia 1980

4 1981–1990

Central African Republic 1981
Ghana 1981
Chad 1982
Burkina Faso 1983, 1987
Nigeria 1983
Guinea 1984
Mauritania 1984
Sudan 1985, 1989
Uganda 1985
Lesotho 1986
Burundi 1987
2 Tunisia 1987
Somalia 1990

5 1991–2000

1 Ethiopia 1991
2 Lesotho 1991, 1993
3 Mali 1991
4 Algeria 1992
5 Chad 1992
6 Sierra Leone 1992, 1997
7 Nigeria 1993
8 Gambia 1994
9 Burundi 1996
10 Niger 1996, 1999
11 Congo, Dem Rep 1997
12 Congo, Republic of 1997
13 Comoros 1999

14 Guinea-Bissau 1999
15 Ivory Coast 1999

© DIAGRAM

Glossary

Allah The Muslim name for God.

animism A belief that phenomena, natural objects, and the universe itself all possess souls.

BCE Before Common Era.

caliph The temporal and religious leader of the Islamic world. The word in Arabic means "successor," as the first caliph was Muhammad's father-in-law, Abu Bakr, the first of the "Four Rightly-Guided Caliphs." When Islam split into Shi'ah and Sunni branches, the caliphate (the central ruling office of caliph) passed to the Sunni Ommayad and Abbasid dynasties, and then the Mamluks of Egypt. After the Ottoman conquest of Egypt in 1517, the title was assumed by the Ottoman sultans until it was abolished in 1924.

cataract Rock-strewn stretch of river making navigation impossible.

CE Common Era.

Christianity Religion founded by Jesus Christ at the start of the Common Era. Christians believe that Jesus was the son of God and the Messiah, or anointed one, who was promised to the Jews by God. His arrival marked the beginning of God's kingdom on Earth.

Copts The Christian people of Egypt and Ethiopia; their language is called Coptic.

corsair A pirate sanctioned or approved by the government or authorities of his home port.

dynasty Ruling family in which power passes, usually from father to son, over generations.

empire A collection of different peoples and territories, often of large area, under the rule of one person or country.

fundamentalism A movement that is part of a larger group which favors strict observance of the group's basic principles and ideas.

hieratic A condensed and simplified form of hieroglyphics used by scribes in Ancient Egypt to write less important documents.

hieroglyphics A form of writing used in Ancient Egypt which uses pictures and symbols to represent concepts, objects, or sounds.

imperialism Either the policy, or the practice, of extending the rule of one state over other, formerly independent, territories.

imam A Muslim religious leader, who often leads prayers at a mosque.

Islam Religion founded by Muhammad after 622 CE with the main belief that there is only one God, and that Muhammad was his prophet; the Qur'an is the holy book of Islam.

Maghrib Name for the region comprising Morocco, Algeria, and Tunisia.

mahout An Islamic preacher.

mercenary A soldier who does not fight for patriotism, but for money.

monarchy A system of government in which supreme power is vested in the single, hereditary figure of a king or queen.

monastery The residence of a religious community, especially of monks, living in seclusion from the rest of the world; such a system is known as monasticism.

mosque A Muslim place of worship.

Muslim A believer in Islam.

mya Million years ago.

nomads People who move or wander from place to place in search of pasture, food, water, or trade; the word derives from the Latin *nomas*, or wandering shepherd.

pastoralist A person who raises livestock.

pharaoh The title of the kings of Ancient Egypt.

puppet ruler A ruler who appears to be independent but is in fact controlled by another, often foreign, country or ruler

Qur'an The holy book of Islam.

republic A form of government in which the people, or their elected representatives, possess supreme power and elect their head of state.

sharia Islamic holy law, a body of doctrines and laws that regulate the lives of those who profess Islam.

Shi'ah The followers of Islam who believe that only the descendants of Muhammad's daughter Fatima, and her husband Ali, should succeed him. After Ali's death, God sent *imams* descended from Ali as his infallible messengers.

Sunni The followers of Islam who accept the authority of the Sunna, the code of behavior based on Muhammad's words and deeds. They believe that the caliphs who succeeded him were his rightful successors.

viceroy A governor of a colony or province of an empire who acts on behalf of the imperial ruler.

Tutankhamun's mask
This beautifully engraved mask, fashioned out of gold, covered the face of the mummy belonging to the boy-king Tutankhamun. He was a pharaoh who died more than 3,300 years ago at the age of 18.

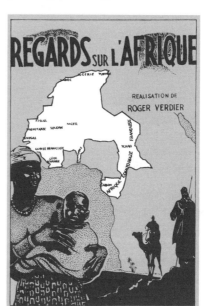

Imperialism
France claimed authority over large areas of northwest Africa, a situation reflected in this movie poster from the 1930s.

© DIAGRAM

Bibliography

Adams, Richard H., *Development and Social Change in Rural Egypt,* Syracuse, New York: Syracuse University Press (1986)

Adams, William Y., *Nubia: Corridor to Africa,* Princeton, N. J.: Princeton University Press (1984)

Arkell, Anthony J., *History of the Sudan,* Westport, Conn: Greenwood (1973)

Baines, John & Malek, Jaromir, *Cultural Atlas of Ancient Egypt,* Rev. ed. New York: Facts On File (2002)

Boase, W., *A Closer Look at Egypt,* London: Hamish Hamilton (1977)

Bourguet, Pierre M. du, *Coptic Art,* London: Methuen (1971)

Chatty, D., *From Camel to Truck: the Bedouin in the Modern World,* New York: Vantage Press (1986)

Cornell, Tim and Matthews, John, *Atlas of the Roman World,* New York: Facts On File (1982)

Diagram Group, *African History On File,* New York: Facts On File (2003)

Diagram Group, *Encyclopedia of African Nations,* New York: Facts On File (2002)

Diagram Group, *Encyclopedia of African Peoples,* New York: Facts On File (2000)

Diagram Group, *Peoples of North Africa,* New York: Facts On File (1997)

Diagram Group, *Religions On File,* New York: Facts On File (1990)

Diagram Group, *Timelines On File, 4 vols.* New York: Facts On File (2000)

Hagg, T., *Nubian Culture Past and Present,* Stockholm: Almqvist and Wiksell International (1987)

Hayes, Joyce L., *Nubia,* Boston: Museum of Fine Arts (1992)

Holt, Peter M. & Daly, M.W., *The History of the Sudan,* 5th ed. New York: Longman (2000)

Kamil, Jill, *Coptic Egypt,* Cairo, Egypt: American University in Cairo Press (1987)

Lepidus, Ira M., *A History of Islamic Societies,* 2nd ed. New York: Cambridge University Press (2002)

Middle East and North Africa 1996, 42nd ed. London: Europa Publications (1995)

Robinson, Francis, *Atlas of the Islamic World,* New York: Facts On File (1982)

Rogge, J., *Too Many, Too Long: Sudan's Twenty-year Refugee Problem,* Totowa, New Jersey: Rowman & Allenheid (1985)

Sertima, I., van, ed. *Golden Age of the Moor,* New Brunswick, Canada: Transaction Publishers (1992)

Smith, W. Stevenson, *The Art and Architecture of Ancient Egypt,* New Haven Conn.: Yale University Press (1998)

Trimingham, J. Spencer, *The Influence of Islam Upon Africa,* New York: Longman (1986)

Vantini, Giovanni, *Christianity in the Sudan,* Bologna, Italy: EMI (1981)

Weekes, R.V., ed. *Muslim Peoples: a World Ethnographic Survey,* 2nd ed.,Westport, CT.: Greenwood Press (1984)

Index

Index

Index